Scandal, Salvation and Suffrage

The Amazing Women of the Temperance Movement

Ros Black.

Ros Black

*This book is dedicated
to women everywhere –
let **her story** be told*

Also by Ros Black

A Talent for Humanity – the Life and Work of Lady Henry Somerset
Duxhurst – Surrey's Lost Village

Contents

Acknowledgements

I have been helped by so many people in my research. It never fails to surprise me how generous people are with their time, knowledge and encouragement.

I must firstly pay tribute to Audrey Ward for awakening my interest in Lady Henry Somerset and setting me off on an incredible journey of discovery. I am indebted to Dr Annemarie McAllister of the University of Central Lancashire (UCLAN) for her enthusiasm for the temperance movement and for a wonderful re-enactment of a Band of Hope Meeting at the People's History Museum, Manchester. Her colleague, Helen Cooper, curator of the Livesey Collection at UCLAN was also most helpful. Temperance historians and academics including Cynthia Belaskie have pointed me in some useful directions..

I have found staff at libraries and local history centres unfailingly helpful. My local Haywards Heath library has ordered in many books for me. The British Library, as always, has proved a rich source of pleasure and knowledge. Staff at Portsmouth History Centre, the Surrey History Centre, the Plymouth and West Devon Records Office and The National Archives at Kew have provided valuable assistance. I have been granted full access to the archives at The Institute of Alcohol Studies in London, where staff were very friendly and encouraging. Personnel at the Salvation Army International Heritage Centre and Lambeth Palace Library were similarly most obliging.

Much, but not all, of the story of women and the temperance movement is linked to the history of the British Women's Temperance Association. Today's successor organization is most commonly known as The White Ribbon Association and staff at its

Solihull archives have been wonderfully generous with their time, resources and knowledge, particularly Anna Homer, Mary Ayres, Gail Williams and Victoria Taylor-Smith.

In researching Sarah Robinson's story, I was assisted by Jane Seabrook, local historian & bookshop owner in East Hoathly. Through the wonders of the internet I have been contacted by relatives of Sarah now living in South Africa, including Ashton Emery. The Davis family of Swartberg and the Solomon family from near Howick have shared with me the delights of one of Sarah's original journals.

The story of Agnes Weston took me to Plymouth. Nigel Overton of Plymouth Museum was most helpful and through him I was also assisted by Alston Kennerley of Plymouth University and Graham Brooks of the Plymouth Postcard Club. Local residents John Elder and Pippa Clewer, who both have links to the old Royal Sailors' Rests, have kindly shared with me family stories which have helped bring Agnes's story to life and made me appreciate what a legacy she has left. The National Museum of the Royal Navy at Portsmouth was also a useful source of information.

The same people who assisted me with my original researches in to the life of Lady Henry Somerset, for my first book, also deserve mention here, particularly Eileen Wood, curator of Reigate Priory Museum, James Hervey-Bathurst, owner of Eastnor Castle, Hazel Lein, archivist at Eastnor, Surrey historians Alan Moore, Sean Hawkins, Mary Slade and Carolyn Burnley and the current and former residents of Duxhurst. Arthur and Pauline Kennedy provided some fascinating photographs. I had assistance from across the Atlantic regarding Lady Henry's great friend Frances Willard, especially from Janet Olsen and Mary McWilliams and from academics Carolyn De Swarte Gifford and Olwen Niessen.

I was granted access to the archives at Castle Howard, by kind permission of the Hon. Simon Howard. The Assistant Curator,

Anna-Louise Mason, and Curator, Dr Christopher Ridgway, have been very helpful.

Without the support of family and friends it would be impossible to write any book. I salute you all.

Particular mention must go to my friends at Sutton Writers who gave me valuable feedback regarding titles and cover design and to Lena Scott who kindly provided a very long term loan of a most useful book.

Special thanks to Rosemary Callinan and Steve Black for their constructive comments on the draft manuscript.

Introduction

The women featured in this book didn't necessarily think of themselves as feminists, yet their stories provide wonderful examples of what females could achieve. As we delve into the murky depths of the temperance movement, we find a colourful collection of female stars – women who didn't let the lack of a vote affect their desire to highlight the perils of the drinking culture and to help others. Through their biographies, we can see how the movement impinged upon many aspects of life in the 19th and early 20th centuries.

History hasn't been kind to the temperance crusade; it is either ignored or ridiculed. Its proponents are often perceived as cranks rather than as champions of social change. Yet it was a huge campaign, at its height in the late Victorian era. We think of prohibition as a somewhat bizarre, short-lived American experiment, spawning bootlegger heroes for page and screen. It could never have happened in Britain.

Or could it? In fact, Scotland came close. In 1913, just before the outbreak of the First World War, The Temperance (Scotland) Act was passed, giving voters the right to impose a local veto on the sale of alcohol in their area. Throughout the rest of the United Kingdom, the introduction of severe restrictions on the liquor trade was a very real possibility.

Some women – Sarah Robinson, Agnes Weston, Catherine Booth, Lady Henry Somerset and Rosalind Howard – were very major players and each warrants detailed consideration in this book. Others featured, like Mrs Elizabeth Lewis and Julia Wightman, were important figures, willing to break the mould of subservient womanhood. Two female-led temperance organizations – the Band of Hope, founded in 1847, to encourage children to understand and avoid the perils of alcohol, and the British Women's Temperance Association founded in 1876, to mobilize the women's voice – are central to the story. The timeline in Chapter 1 helps illustrate where our ladies fit into the overall picture. Perhaps not surprisingly, we discover that, from the women's perspective, the campaign for temperance had many links to the campaign for suffrage.

You don't have to be a teetotaller yourself (I'm not) to admire the courage and determination of these women. You don't have to subscribe to the image of 'the demon drink' to enjoy their stories.

I discovered the work of Lady Henry Somerset, a Victorian temperance leader, quite by chance when visiting some local sites open over the annual Heritage Weekend. I had lived for 30 years in Reigate, Surrey, where Lady Henry had had a home. Although I had worked in the field of special needs social housing, I had never been aware that, in the 1890s, Lady Henry had set up a village just south of the town for the rehabilitation of women with alcohol problems. In reality, she had been doing my job over a hundred years before me.

In researching Lady Henry Somerset's story, I came across many other amazing women from her period. Some were content to help individuals in a small way; others felt compelled to campaign on a bigger scale. Many found they had a real way with words, either teaching or writing – both socially acceptable practices. A few espoused temperance as a political cause, as important, perhaps even more important, than women's suffrage. For many, temperance went hand-in-hand with evangelism. Salvation was sought through sobriety.

These women challenged the traditions of the navy, the army and the established church. There were aristocratic ladies, like Lady Henry Somerset and Rosalind Howard, or wives of vicars or preachers, like Catherine Booth or Julia Wightman. There were working class women determined to help children resist the temptations of alcohol through Band of Hope meetings. They weren't 'Lady Bountifuls' – doing their bit for the poorer classes without ever getting their hands dirty. These were women who spent time, energy, and often their own money, to help others in very practical ways. They shared a steely resolve and a willingness to step outside the tight confines of the Victorian class structure.

These women often had their own personal demons – marital difficulties, illness or severe disability – but still they had the courage to work for the greater good of humanity.

But why choose to fight for temperance? Why pick as an enemy the liquor trade, which had great public appeal and significant vested interests? And what exactly were they fighting for – moderation in drinking habits, total abstinence or even prohibition? Could temperance stand alone as an objective or was it intrinsically linked with other burning issues of the day, such as suffrage and the welfare of children?

Each woman featured answered these questions in a different way. Some of them were admirable but not likeable. Others were women ahead of their time. Many were great writers and orators, but also knew that actions speak louder than words. Often the scale and scope of their work was remarkable.

This book is not intended as an academic history of the temperance movement. Such histories as there are focus very much on individual men such as Joseph Livesey, 'the father of teetotalism' or the male-dominated temperance organizations such as the UK Alliance which supported prohibition. The role of women in the campaign has been largely ignored.

Sex, slander and scandal all feature in the stories of these amazing women. I will leave the reader to decide whether there are any lessons to be learnt today from the work of these women. I merely wish to tell their tales and ask the question – do they deserve to be forgotten?

CHAPTER 1

Temperance Times

A TIMELINE

1829   A small temperance society for women established in Maryhill, near Glasgow.

1830   The Beer Act increased the number of outlets for drink as a licence was no longer required for malt beers.

1833   Joseph Livesey delivered his 'Malt Lecture', spawning the teetotal movement.

1837   Queen Victoria came to the throne.

1838   Slavery abolished in the British Empire.

1846   The Corn Laws repealed, making bread cheaper.

1847   Band of Hope founded, educating children about the dangers of alcohol.
       Hours of work of women and children limited to 63 per week.

1854-6 The Crimean War.

1857   The Indian Mutiny.

1859   Julia Wightman's *Haste to the Rescue* published.

1866   Ist petition for women's suffrage, signed by 1,499 eminent women including Florence Nightingale, presented to parliament by John Stuart Mill.

1867   Reform Act extends male franchise.

1867   Some women able to vote in municipal elections.

1870   Women get limited right to retain their property after marriage.

1873   In Ohio, America, women started campaigning for prohibition.

1

1874   Sarah Robinson set up the teetotal Soldiers' Institute in Portsmouth.

1876   British Women's Temperance Association (BWTA) founded.
Agnes Weston opened the teetotal Sailors' Rest in Devonport.

1878   Salvation Army founded by William and Catherine Booth.

1880-1 Ist Boer War.

1881   Agnes Weston opened her Sailors' Rest in Portsmouth.

1883   House of Common's vote on women's suffrage defeated by just 16 votes.
Married women get right to acquire their own property.

1884   Reform Act extends vote to most adult men.

1888   Women get right to vote in County elections.
The Women's Penny Paper, a feminist journal, launched. Name changed in 1891 to *The Woman's Herald*. Bought by Lady Henry Somerset in 1893 and renamed *The Woman's Signal*.

1889   Elizabeth Lewis, a temperance reformer in Blackburn, won her case for slander.

1890   Lady Henry Somerset elected President of the BWTA.

1893   New Zealand becomes 1st country to give women the right to vote in national elections

1893   Split in ranks of BWTA.

1896   Duxhurst, Lady Henry Somerset's farm colony for inebriate women, had royal opening.

1897   National Union of Women's Suffrage Societies (NUWSS) – 'The Suffragists' – formed.

1901   Queen Victoria died, succeeded by Edward VII.

1903   Rosalind Howard, Countess of Carlisle, took over presidency of the renamed National British Women's Temperance Association.

1903   Women's Social & Political Union (WSPU) – 'The Suffragettes' – formed.

1907   Temperance legislation defeated in House of Lords.

1913 The Temperance (Scotland) Act gave voters the right to ban the sale of alcohol in their area. The introduction of similar measures in England was deferred.

1914 Outbreak of WWI – temperance measures imposed in areas of strategic importance. WSPU and NUWSS suspended campaigning to help the war effort.

1915 King Edward VII took the pledge for the duration of the war.

1917 The House of Commons passed a bill which became the

1918 Representation of the People Act giving women of property over 30 and female graduates the right to vote. Voting age for men reduced to 21.

Women given right to stand for parliament.

Constance Markievicz became 1st female to be elected an MP but as a member of Sinn Fein she didn't take up her seat.

Armistice Day 11 November.

1919 Treaty of Versailles officially brought First World War to an end.

Lady Nancy Astor, a temperance supporter, won a by-election and became 1st women to take her seat in the House of Commons.

In America, the 18th Amendment to the Constitution brought in prohibition to all states, making the sale and manufacture of alcohol illegal. This Prohibition Era lasted almost 14 years until December 1933.

1928 Women given same rights to vote as men.

In the Victorian period, alcohol consumption was massive. It was a way of life. Beer was cheaper than bread; spirits were deemed to have 'medicinal' benefits.

We might smile when we read of the jolly capers of Mr Pickwick and his friends but Dickens's books clearly show how deeply embedded drinking was in the social culture of the 19th century. It was one of the few pastimes which transcended class structure. The working man was as keen on his ale as the lord was on his wines and spirits. The vicar liked his port, the sailor his rum – the latter kindly supplied by the navy for services rendered.

Nor was it just the men who drank. Working class women could frequently be found at the pub, sometimes leaving children to care for themselves. Thanks to the Beer Act of 1830 and the introduction of grocers' licences in 1861, it was even easier for women to access drink – it could now be bought at many shops along with the groceries, enabling wives to hide the cost of their drinking habit from their families. Ironically, it had been argued that these measures would reduce drinking because they didn't apply to spirits!

The more sophisticated women, or the city dwellers, might head for the gin palaces. Such women were particularly open to sexual exploitation. Often drinking and prostitution went hand in hand, cause and effect indelibly confused. So it is no surprise that Josephine Butler's campaign for 'social purity' attracted many temperance campaigners, male and female.

To many, alcohol offered a temporary escape from their hard lives. Others thrived on the sensory pleasure it seemed to afford. Upper class, educated ladies, frustrated by their tedious and dull lives, might become the silent, lonely victims of alcoholism.

However, it was the women who usually had to suffer and manage the consequences of excessive drinking by their men folk. It was the women who struggled to keep enough money back from their husbands' pay to feed the family before it was spent at the pub. It was they who had to shelter the children from aggressive drunken fathers, often taking beatings themselves in the process. And it was they who had to watch as sons grew up to regard beer as the staple drink – no fizzy drinks, perhaps not even safe drinking water, at this time.

So working class women in particular were well placed to identify the problems. They were not so well placed to find solutions. But if a middle or upper class woman was kind enough to offer them some support or encouragement, often with Bible and temperance tract in hand, they might easily be persuaded that signing the pledge offered a way out of their predicament. Of course, in reality, life was never that simple. Husbands had to be persuaded of the error of their ways. Pledges were easily broken. But as the century progressed, in many households throughout the land, the message that excessive drinking caused harm to family life started to get through.

In Victorian Britain, the temperance cause was undoubtedly led and dominated by men. Joseph Livesey, a cheesemonger from Preston, is often called 'the father of teetotalism'. He did not believe in moderation but promoted teetotalism as a vehicle for individual self-improvement. In his view, drunkenness could only be prevented if people didn't develop any appetite, whether moderate or excessive, for alcohol. Livesey refuted the argument that beer was healthy with his famous 'malt lecture', where he analysed a glass of ale to show it had little nutritional value and, with a dramatic flourish, set fire to his samples. The lecture was published, reprinted and delivered around the north. Copies were sent to all MPs. Yet Disraeli still referred to beer as 'liquid bread'.

A reformed drunkard could take the high moral ground but he could also be a dramatic example to others of the benefits of renouncing alcohol. Some colourful characters emerged as speakers, as teetotallers toured the north exhorting others to follow their example. Thomas Swindlehurst styled himself 'the King of the Reformed Drunkards'; Thomas Worsnop became 'The Eccentric Advocate', with his rattle, bright flag and general 'loudness'. Such men attracted attention to the cause, even if the middle-class gentlemen of the temperance movement shuddered with distaste at their antics.

Evangelism was spreading as people sought a better way of life.

Itinerant preachers, including visitors from America, would travel the land taking the word of God to those who were not regular church goers. The Salvation Army led the evangelical temperance charge. Its founders, William and Catherine Booth, strongly advocated total abstinence. The growth of journals and the ease at which tracts and speeches could be printed and circulated meant the lessons of the evangelists weren't lost amidst the grind of daily life.

Teetotalism became something of a 'holy cause', with the pledge as the central creed. Temperance advocates and agents were referred to as 'missionaries', reformed drunkards as 'the saved', alcoholic drink was demonised. This is often the image conjured up when temperance is mentioned today and may be the reason why the movement is dismissed as unimportant or irrelevant. Yet the temperance cause, for all its impassioned rhetoric, was bigger and better than this.

The Church of England was slow to become formally involved but ultimately formed the Church of England Temperance Society and even a Church Army, to emulate the Salvation Army. At the Lambeth Palace Conference in 1888, a report was presented which said "The Church should use its utmost influence to press on all governments the duty of diminishing the enormous amount of temptation which at present hinders the work of elevating and civilizing the masses…" But concern was also expressed about the religious zeal of "fanatics" promoting total abstinence.

The Church of England Temperance Society (CETS) formed an auxiliary branch, the Women's Union, employing females to work specifically with women and children. It was generally accepted, at this time, that women inebriates couldn't be cured. But the Women's Union set up homes for female drunkards, with the richer ladies paying fees to stay and the poorer women working in the homes for their keep. This was an idea which Lady Henry Somerset would take much further with Duxhurst, her "farm colony for inebriate women". And, as we shall see, Lady Henry hotly disputed the notion that cure was impossible.

By the late 1860s, the National Temperance League (NTL) was persuaded to support the work being done by Sarah Robinson to improve the welfare of soldiers. This says a lot about the charisma and determination of the redoubtable Miss Robinson. Ironically the NTL's support was a reaction to a very non-supportive article in the press which heaped scorn on '*The Women on the Temperance Platform*'. Soon, the NTL was also supporting the work of Agnes Weston with the navy.

The success of Sarah and Agnes, working under the NTL umbrella, made the League more receptive to the role women could play in the movement. As early as 1872, in its journal, *The Temperance Record*, the NTL paid tribute to the temperance work of Emily Anne Sulivan in Devon and Dorset. In a moving obituary, her "courage, diligence and her extraordinary sympathy" were praised. For Emily had worked with those drunkards whom neighbours, and even clergymen, had said were better avoided because of their violence and insolence. Her womanly touch had won over many converts to temperance. "She was quite at home speaking to 'roughs' but was also the light and life of every drawing room she entered." This was a rare recognition that women could be more effective than men with some people.

Another perceptive comment made about Emily Sulivan concerned her approach to women who had been brought low by alcohol abuse. "She had the largest sympathy with the fallen of her own sex, to whom so often their own sex show themselves the most intolerant."

The British and Foreign Temperance Society (BFTS) allowed women an active part in campaigning. It was no coincidence that this society was heavily supported by various Quakers. For amongst Quakers, women were allowed to take on prominent roles. So Quaker women expected to be seen, and heard, in temperance work. The BFTS attracted some high profile female supporters such as the Duchess of Beaufort and Lady Olivia Sparrow. Queen Victoria became a patron – an important boost to its work. In fact, throughout her long reign, the Queen lent her support to many activities which encouraged moderation in drinking. But she was never a teetotaller herself.

The Quakers, or Society of Friends as they were known, were an international organization. Some, but by no means all, were wealthy. Most practiced teetotalism, though some would drink alcohol in moderation. Most importantly, Quakers had a genuine compassion for all of humanity, whatever their sex, class or occupation.

In America many Quaker women had risen to prominence and they were keen to spread their work across the Atlantic. The visit of Eliza 'Mother' Stewart, to England in 1875 is widely regarded as being the catalyst for the growth of the women's temperance movement in Britain.

Prior to that, the momentum had been in women's work with children.

CHAPTER 2

Anne Jane Carlile and the Band of Hope

The Band of Hope, an umbrella group for a multitude of local branches working with children to teach them the dangers of drinking, could not have flourished without its female workers. It provided a respectable activity for women and children.

"Train up a child in the way he should go and when he is old, he will not depart." This biblical quote, from the Book of Proverbs, became the motto of the Band of Hope. The aims of this movement were very clear. "Catch them young," we would say today. The leaders believed that if children could be taught the perils of alcohol from an early age, then they would not be tempted when older.

On the one hand, it might be seen as indoctrination on a wide scale. On another, it can be seen as a movement which provided social activities for children in a wholesome environment, which kept them off the street and out of harm.

Mrs Anne Jane Carlile is usually credited with founding the Band of Hope, along with the Reverend Jabez Tunnicliff, a Baptist minister. The Reverend would often claim the Band of Hope was his own creation, to the irritation of many female temperance supporters.

Mrs Carlile was the wife of a Presbyterian minister, living in Ireland. She had been active in religious and philanthropic work, including visiting women's prisons, from around 1800. She had worked alongside Elizabeth Fry for several years. She noted that "nearly all who came there [prison] came by drink". Mrs Carlile was a teetaller, who had taken the pledge herself. She sought to promote this in her work with women and children. In an article in *The Irish Times* in 1960, DM Hartford describes Mrs Carlile as "An

Irish pioneer of reform". He describes how she "overcame her own reluctance and the strong feelings of the times against women speakers". The pledge she used read: "I promise, by Divine aid, to abstain from all intoxicating drinks as beverages, and to avoid all participation in drinking customs."

Anne Carlile had come over to England on several occasions, invited to speak at Missions. In 1847, she was making her third visit to England, having been invited by the Leeds Temperance Society for a 10 day visit. One story is that Rev. Tunnicliff had been prompted to invite her because of the words of a dying drunkard in June 1847. On his death bed, the man, once a respected school teacher, cried out to the minister, "Warn young people about the danger of the first glass." In Leeds, Mrs Carlile held meetings in Day Schools, and talked to both Sunday School classes and groups of women. She persuaded many of the teenage lads to sign the pledge.

The Committee of the Leeds Temperance Society, led by the Rev. Tunnicliff, was impressed. Perhaps this work with children was a role for which women were well suited, they decided. They resolved to set up a ladies committee to continue Mrs Carlile's work promoting temperance amongst children. The committee was supervised by Rev. Tunnicliff.

The Reverend later suggested this become a separate organization with a distinct name, 'The Temperance Band of Hope'. Others recorded that Mrs Carlile herself had referred to a 'Band of Hope' as she had been watching the children sing. The phrase was also in use at that time in Germany.

Whatever the origins of the actual name, the organization it spawned became huge. Children as young as six were encouraged to join and to sign the pledge. The original Band of Hope pledge included promising to abstain from all intoxicating liquors and from tobacco in all its forms, but this was soon changed to "I do agree that I will not use intoxicating liquor as a beverage".

This was an important change for two reasons. Firstly the dangers of tobacco were not so strongly appreciated at that time that it was felt necessary to encourage its prohibition amongst the young. But most significantly, it was a recognition that many adults excused drinking 'for medicinal purposes'. It was difficult, and hypocritical, to expect children to renounce all alcohol, if the parents still wanted to pretend their own drinking was for the good of their health. Many parents found themselves encouraging their children to attend Band of Hope meetings because they were generally educational and entertaining but objecting to the pledge the children were required to sign. Worse still, from some parents' perspective, many Band of Hope branches required the parents themselves to take the pledge.

One of the secrets of the success of the Band of Hope was its 'respectability'. Another was its organization. Local Bands of Hope were invited to join a UK Band of Hope Union in 1855. There were newspapers, *The Band of Hope Review* and *The Sunday Scholars' Friend* published by temperance stalwart, TB Smithies. He had taken the pledge from Mrs Carlile and used to refer to her as his "temperance mother".

The Union took on the role of producing songbooks and pledge cards. Over 1,000 temperance talks, especially adapted for children, were published. These were known as 'Blackboard Addresses'. Typical topics were "The Four Pillars of Temperance: Scripture, Reason, Science and Experience" drawn to resemble a classical temple. Or warnings such as

D eadens the Touch
R uins the Taste
I mpairs the Sight
N umbs the Smelling
K ills the Hearing

In the north of England, many of the groups established their own Unions. A new paper, *Onward*, became their official organ – another rich source of stories, songs and sheet music.

Catchy songs and choirs attracted the children and kept them entertained. Ballads such as *Come Home, Father* pulled at the heart strings of the adults. To hear children belting out *The Temperance Anthem*, to the tune of the National Anthem, must have been a stirring experience.

> *"God bless our youthful band, O may we firmly stand True to our pledge;*
> *May we to liberty, Truth, love and charity, Evermore faithful be,*
> *From youth to age."*

Soon the UK Band of Hope Union was holding giant festivals at Crystal Palace, where a choir of over 1,000 children joined together to sing their temperance songs – the pop songs of the day. By 1865, the Union choir had 2,000 members.

Most Band of Hope branches had an annual outing – a great attraction for both children and their parents and possibly one of the prime reasons why so many joined up. The various musical festivals certainly provided opportunities for travel and new experiences.

At its annual conference in 1872, the Band of Hope Union reported some significant results. It had created greater publicity for the temperance movement and claimed to have improved the "moral tone in the general conduct of juveniles" through promoting the virtues of "cleanliness, honesty, veracity, obedience and industry" as well as abstinence from alcohol. There was now a new generation of adults still committed to teetotalism because of their childhood Band of Hope learning. Moreover, many drunkards had "succumbed to the simple eloquence of a little child" and taken the pledge.

The Band of Hope was well supported by other temperance organizations. The Church of England Temperance Society and the

British Women's Temperance Association particularly took pride in encouraging their own members to set up Band of Hope groups for local children. The Catholic Church didn't like the name 'Band of Hope' but they had very similar children's groups.

In 1890, a week-long Band of Hope Grand Bazaar was held at the Exeter Hall in London, opened by Princess Louise. It raised £3,398, an enormous sum for the time, worth over £370,000 today.

The movement continued to grow throughout Britain. By 1889 there were some 16,000 Band of Hope Societies, with over two million members. By 1900, the Band of Hope Union claimed that 10% of all UK children attended Bands of Hope activities – an incredible statistic. So, if you are researching your family history, you may well discover references to Band of Hope meetings; perhaps you might even discover your great grandfather's pledge card.

The majority, though not all, of Band of Hope workers were women. Initially only men were allowed to be actual teachers; women had to work as their assistants. Rev. Tunnicliff and his committee had been proved right. Women were very suited to this work. And the work was very suited to the role women then had in society – working away quietly in the background, doing good, but not stirring up too much trouble!

If any woman wrote a paper for a conference, this had to be delivered by a man. Today this seems outrageous, but in the late 19th century it was the norm. However, women like Clara Lucas Balfour challenged this. She had gained a reputation as an author, penning many temperance stories, with titles such as *Morning Dew-Drops*. She started to write conference papers and she insisted on delivering them herself. Women were beginning to assert themselves and they were using temperance as a vehicle.

The Band of Hope, now Hope UK, still works with children and young people today. The stirring songs may have gone but the aim to raise awareness of drug and alcohol issues lives on.

CHAPTER 3

Julia Wightman (1817 – 1898) – an Early Pioneer

Mrs Julia Wightman was, in many ways, typical of the women who got involved in the temperance movement in the 1850s. Her book, *Haste to the Rescue*, brought renewed impetus to women's work for temperance reform. She was the wife of a clergyman, trying to help out parishioners at a local level rather than aiming to tackle the excesses of liquor trade in any political or national way.

Initially she regarded the temperance pledge as "an absurdity", though this didn't stop her trying to get people to sign it. She was really a moderationist. "Why should not men drink moderately and exercise self-control?" she argued.

But as she continued her work in the parish, holding cottage meetings for tea, chat and Bible readings, she realized that even moderate drinking could cause problems. She saw that it was only by abstaining totally that men stood a chance of reforming. In her view, drunkenness was a stumbling-block to finding God. For Julia, religion came first; temperance second.

She also recognized, "Total abstinence is not a cure for drunkenness but only holds it in abeyance so long as it is strictly adhered to." Hence why the pledge was so important. Julia was also sceptical about the perceived benefits of alcohol for health.

Shrewsbury, where Julia lived, was a garrison town and Julia witnessed how the soldiers would receive their pay, then immediately go and spend it on drink. When the volunteer militia were called up, the men were billeted in pubs, temptation almost forced down their throats.

She argued that too many men – some 60,000 a year – died from alcohol-related causes, far more than our casualties in the Crimea and India. Yet fatalities in wars were much more in the nation's consciousness.

Her work might have remained purely local if she hadn't been persuaded by her friends to write about her experiences. *Haste to the Rescue*, published in 1859, proved a surprising success. In the first 14 months after its publication, 26,000 copies had been circulated. Yet the book had been quickly put together, based on letters Julia had written to her sister and to a friend about her work.

It seems the public were surprised that a woman was doing this sort of work, trying to reform and rehabilitate drunkards. They were keen to learn more and a second book, *Annals of the Rescued*, was produced, selling 6,000 copies.

The profits from the books were ploughed into setting up "a public-house without the drink" in Shrewsbury, to give the working men somewhere they could meet for recreational purposes; "where cheerfulness and social intercourse may be enjoyed after their day's work". The hall soon housed a church ragged school; in the evenings there would be Bible classes for policemen and postmen. It became a real hub of the community.

Julia was very keen to use other women to help in her work. The feminine touch often seemed effective when the no-nonsense approach of a man didn't. "They say a lady can manage a rough horse better than a man," she wrote in *Haste to the Rescue*. "Perhaps it may be the same with these men [drunkards], for, rough as they seem, the very gentlest influence tells most on them – it melts and wins them …"

Her concluding battle-cry, "Women of England, if no-one else will take up this subject as it deserves, will you do so?" struck a chord in the hearts of women throughout England. It was aimed mainly at middle and upper class ladies, to inspire them to convert working class drunkards to both temperance and Christianity. As a direct consequence of Julia's book, many local ladies' associations were formed to do similar work.

She was invited to present a paper at the National Temperance League's conference in 1872. There she told the story of 'Molly', who had been notorious as the nuisance of the neighbourhood, constantly drunk and disorderly, always begging. But Julia had invited her into her own home. She had talked and prayed with her. Molly had seemed struck by the kindness; something she was not used to. The next day, she'd come voluntarily to the vicarage to sign the pledge. With constant encouragement, Molly had started to attend church and forsake her old ways. Julia had been thrilled to host a small tea party to celebrate Molly's first year as a teetotaller; an example of one life turned around by temperance teaching.

Haste to the Rescue also had an impact upon men. WS Caine, who later became an MP, claimed it was Julia's book which converted him to the temperance cause. He said he took the book "to the commercial room of a neighbouring hotel, ordered half a pint of sherry (!) and proceeded to absorb both. It was my last taste of alcohol, and my first of the total abstinence movement". Caine would subsequently be very active in supporting temperance legislation. He served as vice president of the UK Alliance and as president of both the British Temperance League and the National Temperance Federation. And all this through the influence of a woman.

Inevitably, Julia faced criticism – she was doing work which should be done by a man; her place was at home; many of her converts only went along with her teaching because there were practical benefits, like food and warm shelter. But her status as the wife of a clergyman earned her respect. Her words, spoken and written, proved inspirational to many and her practical philanthropy changed lives.

CHAPTER 4

Margaret Bright Lucas (1818 – 1890) and the British Women's Temperance Association

Undoubtedly, the British women's temperance movement was greatly influenced by thinking across the Atlantic. There the single issue of temperance had widened into a whole spectrum of women's issues – suffrage, economic and religious rights, the importance of the home and family.

It had all started in a small way, in Hillsboro, Ohio. In 1873, women marched through the town, stopping at every saloon and making a big show of praying for the souls of the owners and their customers. They even urged bar owners to sign a pledge not to sell alcohol – rather a big ask! The women would go to court houses en masse and kneel and pray. Over the next two years, similar marches were held in over 130 other northern American towns. "It looked as though we were going to take over the world," Eliza Stewart would later write.

Eliza took a high profile role in these protests. She had taken an active part during the American Civil War, helping to set up hospitals and working as a nurse, alongside campaigning roles for the Soldiers' Aid Society and the United States Sanitary Commission. She was used to public attention and, perhaps after the end of the Civil War, she needed a new outlet for her energies. The temperance campaign provided it. Eliza founded area temperance leagues in Ohio and then helped establish the Woman's Christian Temperance Union (WCTU), a national organization. (The American style was to use 'woman' in the singular.)

Even in the 1870s there was already a constant stream of wealthy, well educated women travelling to and from the States. Margaret Parker, a temperance speaker from Dundee, travelled over, keen to find out about the Ohio campaign. She was incredibly impressed. Margaret Barrow, author of a thesis *Temperate Feminists* describes her as being "enamoured by both the WCTU and the American way of life".

On her return to England, Margaret Parker and her friend, and fellow Quaker, Margaret Bright Lucas, issued a call to arms. Women from all over Great Britain and Ireland were invited to attend a meeting in Newcastle. Over 150, many from Scotland, attended. Some represented small local temperance groups already in existence. Eliza Stewart came over to England to lend her voice and experience to the invigorated campaign. The British Women's Temperance Association (BWTA) was born.

The preamble to the BWTA's constitution declared: "In the spirit of Christ, and in the love of God and of humanity, we women of this nation, conscious of the great evils, and appalled by the great dangers of intemperance, band ourselves together for the promotion of Total Abstinence, and the entire extinction of the Liquor Traffic" – a bold and somewhat sweeping objective.

It was an objective which would be interpreted differently by succeeding presidents, some more pragmatic than others. Margaret Parker, the first president, clearly wanted the BWTA to emulate the Woman's Christian Temperance Union (WCTU), its American counterpart – to push for prohibition and to campaign on a whole range of 'women's issues'. Yet, even at this early stage of its development, not all members of the newly formed association agreed with her. This tension would split the BWTA apart less than 20 years later. It may well be one of the reasons why the women's temperance movement didn't gain the recognition it deserved.

"Miserable cowardice, born of unbelief" – that was the reason many women didn't take an active role in public life, claimed Mrs Forsaith, a delegate at the BWTA's annual conference in 1886. "We like to call this sort of thing by nice names, 'shyness', 'timidity', almost a feminine grace, and our gentlemen relatives take care to foster the delusion."

This quotation aptly sums up the social mores of the late Victorian period, with its rigid social hierarchy. Feminism was just a faint glimmer in a male-dominated world. For the upper and middle class woman, campaigning for social reform or political rights was considered 'unladylike'. For the working class woman, the constant battles of daily life – putting meals on the table and caring for the family – meant there was little time or energy for fighting a wider war on living conditions and culture.

However, the formation of the BWTA in 1876 gave some formal structure to the women's role in the temperance issue. Soon the Association became known simply as 'The British Women'. Ironically, the women themselves recognized that they could achieve more by setting up local groups and concentrating less on the national picture. So the BWTA was initially a very loose structure, an umbrella group for many county or town based branches. However, there was strong agreement that the women's temperance movement was a Christian one – though non-denominational. All meetings would open and close with prayer.

The first president of the BWTA, Margaret Parker, was succeeded by Clara Lucas Balfour, a well known author of temperance tracts. Clara was determined that women should take a more active role in society and that their voices should be heard. Sadly health problems meant her tenure as president lasted just one year.

Margaret Bright Lucas, one of the original founders, then took over and led the association for the next 12 years. Margaret was the sister of the Anti-Corn Law reformer and MP, John Bright. The Brights were a strong Quaker family with liberal politics. Margaret married her cousin, Samuel Lucas, who went on to become the owner and editor of *The Morning Star*, a radical newspaper. During the early years of their marriage, the couple had some financial difficulties but life was much improved when Margaret's father settled a considerable sum of money on her.

Margaret had participated, in a low key way, in her brother's campaigns. As early as 1866, she had signed the first women's suffrage petition to the House of Commons, asking for the vote for unmarried women and widows. Yet she didn't really become politically active in her own right until after her husband's death, when her two children were grown up and themselves married.

Then she put her financial, and personal, independence to good use. It was almost as though she had to make up for lost time. She made a long visit to the States, enjoying the company of many Quakers and learning more about American temperance politics. On her return, she joined, and reached high office, in many organizations. In 1872 she became a member of the Independent Order of the Good Templars (IOGT). By 1875 she had reached the level of 'grand worthy vice templar', the highest honour conferred by the IOGT on a British woman. Although the Good Templars, with their colourful regalia, might seem an odd match for Quakers, the two groups shared many of the same values. Many Quakers became very active in the IOGT. Women certainly enjoyed more equality within the IOGT and were allowed, even encouraged, to speak in public, something at which Margaret became very adept. In a history of the temperance movement written in 1897, the IOGT was credited with "setting free a great amount of latent feminine power for temperance".

Margaret became vice president of the National Temperance Federation and the first female vice president of the UK Alliance, strongly supporting prohibition.

She espoused many of the social reform causes of the day. She supported Josephine Butler's work and accompanied her to the

Geneva International Convention on the Contagious Diseases Acts. She also became president of the Women's Peace and Arbitration Association and vice president of The Peace Society. She served on the executive committee of the Women's Liberal Association.

Frances Willard, the American temperance leader and founder of the World Woman's Christian Temperance Union (WWCTU), persuaded Margaret to become the WWCTU's first president. This gave her a strong voice on the international stage and led to more visits to the United States. It was following a visit by Margaret to Belgium that a Ladies Temperance Society was formed in Antwerp.

In 1878, Margaret Bright Lucas was the obvious choice to succeed Clara Lucas Balfour as president of the BWTA. She made some significant changes to the association, moving its headquarters from the northeast down to London, so as to be nearer Parliament. In 1879 she presented the first women's petition in favour of Sunday Closing to the House of Commons. She remained close friends with Margaret Parker and the two women frequently travelled together, giving talks. Mrs Parker's son later wrote, "Many went to their meetings out of curiosity but were surprised to see two homely British women ... who had been strengthened by life's responsibilities, who, neither in dress, speech, nor manner, offended against taste or prejudice." The pair weren't 'unwomanly' or eccentric. They certainly weren't cranks.

Under Margaret's presidency, the BWTA moved up a gear. It was boosted when the Yorkshire Women's Christian Temperance Union affiliated to its ranks. In Leeds, one member of the local branch acted as a police court missionary, the forerunners of the probation service. They also assisted other organizations with similar objectives, for example helping the Salvation Army set up a 'Women's Hotel'.

Scottish members decided to form their own Scottish Christian Union under the presidency of Mrs Blaikie, whose husband was

Professor of Theology at Edinburgh University. The links between the English and Scottish women's associations remained strong.

The NTL, which had already shown its support for individual female temperance campaigners, became more vocal in its recognition of the important role women could play. BWTA members started to speak on NTL platforms. By 1882, the NTL was urging women to do more for the cause just by running their household differently. "If every woman in England were to resolve she would never knowingly tempt anybody [with intoxicating drink], and also make a point of offering some other beverage, in the place of intoxicants ... there would soon be a great change in our drinking customs."

In 1884, the BWTA appointed an organizing agent with a specific remit to extend its work and establish at least a further 100 branches. Yet it didn't ignore the more domestic side of a woman's life. *The British Women's Temperance Journal*, official paper of the BWTA, would print handy household hints and recipes such as that for "mince pies without cider, brandy or vinegar". Later the Association even published *The Non-Alcoholic Cookery Book*.

Margaret Bright Lucas always believed that women had superior moral virtues. She recognized that their voice for reform in all women's issues could best be met if they achieved the right to vote. In 1885, the BWTA produced a paper on the political responsibilities of women. The fact that women didn't have the vote didn't mean they shouldn't show an interest in politics, was its theme. Women should influence their men folk to vote for candidates who supported temperance legislation. Although there was a grudging admission that not all women actually wanted the vote, temperance and women's suffrage were now firmly hand-in-hand.

CHAPTER 5

Elizabeth Lewis (1843 – 1924) 'The Drunkard's Friend'

Amongst the ranks of the BWTA was Mrs Elizabeth Lewis of Blackburn. Her story proves that you didn't have to spearhead a national organisation in order to have a real impact.

In fact, the law of the land was changed because of Elizabeth. She was the victim of slander by a local publican. He spread rumours about her "moral integrity". But because she was a woman, unless she could prove financial loss as a result of the slander, she had no right of redress. In 1889, imputations of unchastity or adultery weren't actionable. But Elizabeth was determined to fight to clear her name, employing one of the country's top QCs, Mr Gully.

In the event, as we shall see, the case was settled with the defendant withdrawing his comments and Elizabeth receiving 40 shillings damages and £50 towards her costs. But Mr Gully was also a liberal MP (later elevated to the peerage as Viscount Selby). He was so appalled at the iniquitous treatment of Elizabeth that he proposed, and secured, the passing of *The Slander of Women Act 1891*. This legislation gave women new rights. "The false and malicious speaking and publishing of words which impute unchastity to an unmarried woman, or adultery to a married woman, shall be actionable without proof of specific damage."

Equality of the sexes certainly came in small stages. But this was a real victory and it had all come about because of one woman's role in the temperance movement.

Teetotalism had brought Elizabeth's parents together, when her mother had heard her father speak on the subject in Blackburn. The family felt so strongly about the dangers of alcohol that they wouldn't take communion at their own chapel – because fermented wine was used. Elizabeth was a keen member of the local Band of Hope, singing in its choir.

When she married, it was to a local coach builder who shared her views on temperance. The couple joined the Order of the Good Templars (IOGT) in Blackburn in 1872 and both held office within the group. 10 years later, Mrs Parker and Mrs Bright Lucas formed a branch of the BWTA in Blackburn and Elizabeth and her mother were amongst its first members.

A Blue Ribbon Gospel Temperance mission was held in the town and Elizabeth sat on the platform with her husband, who was on the organizing committee. Although she didn't address the meeting directly, Elizabeth managed "in fear and trembling" to go out into the body of the meeting and take pledges. Her first effort at public speaking later that week was a disaster. She stood there speechless and in tears.

One-to-one counselling, however, was something she could do. She went to visit some of the people who had signed the pledge and she quickly realized how important follow-up work was with these men and women. So, encouraged by her husband, she took a bold step. She employed a missionary, Mr Kilshaw, to continue the work of the Blue Ribbon mission, to assist her with visiting houses and holding meetings. Richard Kilshaw was very much a working-class man, someone to whom others could relate. Mrs Lewis took on sole responsibility for paying his wages.

Soon she started what she called 'Penny Readings', evenings of songs and recitals. Mr Kilshaw would play the banjo; Elizabeth's husband played the cornet. These were advertised in the local paper: "Temperance entertainment in the Spinners' Institute ... admission

1d … All people wishing to spend a pleasant evening are earnestly invited to attend. Pledges taken at close."

One of the features of these weekly meetings was the testimonies of reformed women. Elizabeth very much promoted the idea that becoming a teetotaller was a way of bettering yourself. The tales of these reformed women, of how, now sober, they had been able to rescue their parents from the workhouse, inspired many to sign the pledge. Anything which kept people out of that dreaded Victorian institution had to be a good thing in the audience's mind.

Elizabeth also took to meeting women being discharged from institutions, providing them with openings for work and with suitable lodging. She encouraged all those who had signed the pledge to become involved in the work and activities of the mission; she created a new, supportive community for them – an alternative to the pub.

Elizabeth seemed quite comfortable in the slums, armed with a strong belief that her teetotal ways were the answer to many of the social problems she encountered there. She was quite happy to personalize her arguments, declaring "I am a teetotaller for my own sake, because I am healthier, stronger and better without it. I am a teetotaller because it enables me to go with kind loving words to the poor drunkards and help to free them from their terrible bondage … I am a teetotaller because strong drink is the greatest curse of our land; it is the stumbling block to all Christian, philanthropic work …" Somehow, she seems to have avoided the perils of appearing patronizing to the poor.

It wasn't just words though. Elizabeth brought practical assistance to the poor and to social outcasts. On hearing about one man who had broken his pledge, she searched all the pubs until she found him. She took him back home to his wife and stayed there until after closing time, so he couldn't go out again. The next day she went to his house and walked with him to work. She was at the factory gates to meet him after the end of his shift to take him back to his home and then to her mission meeting. She kept this routine up for weeks until she felt the man was better able to resist temptation.

By the middle of 1883, Elizabeth had overcome her timidity at public speaking. When she laid the foundation stone of a new church at Witton, she was accompanied by a brass band and a 400 strong procession. *The Blackburn Times* referred to her work as "Mrs Lewis's Temperance Mission." As her biographer, and second missionary, WE Moss commented, this lent "a certain formality" to her efforts.

Elizabeth was wise enough to know that she needed to be scrupulously open and honest about her financial dealings. In September 1884, she produced a report of her first year's work. The mission had 80 subscribers, including four MPs and had raised over £72. This, together with the proceeds from a big town hall concert, had been used to pay Mr Kilshaw's wages of 30 shillings per week. It had also paid the printing costs of the many temperance tracts handed out. The balance was carried over. Each year, a similar report would be produced.

Sadly, this didn't protect her from some false accusations. In December 1885, she felt compelled to write to *The Blackburn Times*, denying "emphatically" that she was paid for her work or the work carried out in her name. Her husband's coach building firm began to suffer, as publicans and brewers took their business away. Preaching teetotalism didn't make you popular with the liquor trade.

Elizabeth was living and working in the north east of England, in the heartland of the teetotal movement inspired by Joseph Livesey. She must have been flattered to learn that her hero had heard of her work. In 1884, when Livesey was in failing health, Elizabeth went to visit him. It was Livesey who gave her the sobriquet, "The Drunkard's Friend". He also apparently told her, "Thank God there is someone left to carry on the work on the old lines." It seems the father of teetotalism had made a woman his heir apparent! In her address at Livesey's funeral, Elizabeth pledged to carry on his work.

Encouraged by Livesey's endorsement, Elizabeth became bolder in her campaigning. She decided she needed to go to the top – to the Prime Minister, William Gladstone. She chose to waylay him and his wife at a church near their home, requesting a meeting to discuss the temperance issue, most specifically as it pertained to women. Not surprisingly, Gladstone replied that he was too busy, but his wife agreed to receive Elizabeth that afternoon. Her plea for the abolition of grocers' licences fell on deaf ears, though Mrs Gladstone subsequently sent a donation of one guinea to the mission. Undeterred, Elizabeth lobbied other cabinet ministers. She had certainly come a long way from that tearful first attempt at public speaking.

She would travel round the north of England giving temperance talks. Her work was described in *Alliance News* as "a capital illustration of what an earnest, devoted lady can accomplish without an elaborate organization". In 1885, she even started holding temperance meetings in the huts where the navvies working on the railway line were housed. Her reputation spread. She travelled to Belfast and London to give talks. She was honoured to be asked to chair a special temperance meeting being addressed by Thomas Whittaker, a renowned temperance reformer and one of Livesey's 'disciples'.

Elizabeth was beginning to attract some good publicity. *The Manchester Guardian* published a piece about her work, *The Social Effects of Temperance*. When the editor of *The Blackburn Standard* published a booklet *Sunlight in the Slums, or a day with Mrs Lewis, an account of temperance work in Blackburn's back alleys and courts*, this was widely circulated. The fact that the writer wasn't a teetotaller himself added weight to his eyewitness account. Her message that "alcohol unfits people for their daily work" was being spread far and wide.

Then suddenly all the positive publicity turned to notoriety. Elizabeth had been visiting Blackpool, accompanied by Mr Moss. He was a young, local man whom she had appointed as her missionary, to replace the faithful Mr Kilshaw, who had retired on health grounds. By coincidence, the licensee of the Blackburn pub outside of which she had held many open-air meetings was also in Blackpool, taking a short holiday. On seeing Mrs Lewis and Mr Moss he made some unsavoury comments to his companions. Then, on his return home to Blackburn, he spread rumours about the pair.

Elizabeth was horrified. She and her husband took legal advice. Through some contacts at the UK Alliance, she secured the services of Mr Gully QC, a leading expert on slander. He prepared a case on the basis that, as his client was responsible for the missionary's wages and the mission's expenses, she was likely to suffer a pecuniary loss because of these false accusations.

The judge was not convinced by the defendant's denial that he had ever made such comments. He took the unusual step of asking to hear Elizabeth's version of events before deciding that there was sufficient evidence for the case to proceed. At this point, the defendant probably knew he was beaten, especially as there were witnesses to his remarks. So he offered to settle, withdrawing "all imputations and charges which the words he used may be supposed to have conveyed" – a fairly hollow apology. Whilst denying some of the more offensive expressions, he admitted he had used language which "cast discredit on Mrs Lewis". The judge therefore directed the jury to find for Mrs Lewis. Her supporters, which included many temperance stalwarts, were delighted. A special fund, to cover the costs not met by the court award, was set up by the British Women's Temperance Association, headed by Lady

Henry Somerset. In a clear demonstration of female solidarity, Lady Henry later visited Blackburn to speak at a meeting organized by Elizabeth.

With her reputation fully restored, perhaps even enhanced, by the court case, Elizabeth continued with her work. The Spinners Institute was now too small to accommodate the flourishing temperance meetings. Elizabeth's husband, one of her most steadfast supporters, built a new venue over his carriage works' showroom. The new Lees Hall attracted prominent speakers from around Britain. Although she now had this splendid, purpose-built hall, Elizabeth still enjoyed open-air meetings and found these remained popular.

The pledge wording she used was interesting: "I promise to Abstain from all Intoxicating Drink (and Wine) and will try to induce others to do the same." Here was recognition that teetotallers had a duty to try to convert others to their cause.

At Lees Hall, there were also special women-only meetings, discussing domestic, health and sexual matters. Elizabeth advocated starting married life free from debt, and preferably not until the age of 25.

The Band of Hope group which she had established in the early days of her mission went from strength to strength. She would get the children to chant, "A little drink does a little harm, more drink does more harm, much drink does much harm; so we will never touch it."

The National Temperance League (NTL) was eager to make use of Elizabeth. Its secretary, Robert Rae, visited Blackburn to see her work at first hand, writing an article about it in the NTL's *Weekly Record*. When the NTL launched its national pledge-signing campaign in 1895, Elizabeth was very involved. Missionaries from the World Woman's Christian Temperance Union also visited.

When her husband retired from his coach building business, he joined Elizabeth in her work. But it was Elizabeth who still took the lead in this area of their life. When the King and Queen visited Blackburn in 1913, Elizabeth was one of the people invited to be presented to them.

She was a strong advocate of women's suffrage. "I object as a woman to be classed for voting purposes with lunatics and criminals. Women know what is best for their own sex, and I am positive that if they had the vote they would use it on the side of temperance," she declared. Whilst she was not really in favour of the militancy of the suffragettes, she did allow the local group to use Lees Hall free of charge.

Right up until her death in 1924, Elizabeth remained committed to the temperance cause. "The longer I live," she wrote in 1913, "the more certain I am that our movement lies at the foundation of all social reform."

The work of one woman deeply affected those she met. Her practical kindness, her energy and enthusiasm were an example others strove to emulate. She was a champion of the poor, a true friend of the drunkard and a woman to whom we all owe a debt of gratitude. For if Elizabeth Lewis had allowed herself to be defamed without seeking legal redress, how long would women have had to wait for that change in the law; a change which allowed them equal redress to men for slurs on their morals.

CHAPTER 6

Sarah Robinson (1834 – 1921) 'The Soldiers' Friend'

Picture the scene: a gypsy caravan and a huddle of assorted tents and marquees in the middle of Dartmoor; the banner of the National Temperance League fluttering in the wind; an open camp full of volunteer soldiers on manoeuvres; a woman in charge, disabled with a spinal condition, her pain made worse by the cramped conditions and short bunk bed in the caravan.

For nine long weeks in the autumn of 1873, Sarah Robinson and her team of ten male helpers dispensed coffee, tea, lemonade, cakes and biscuits, all in pennyworths, to the soldiers. Why? Because otherwise they would have had little to drink except beer. And because Sarah was a woman with a lifelong affection for soldiers.

Sarah moved on to Staffordshire with her caravan and tents as other regiments carried out exercises on Cannock Chase. As well as tea and snacks, these temperance workers sold over 7,000 one penny stamps and organized the sending home not just of letters but money – something the army hadn't thought to do. Sarah became so crippled by her experiences in that caravan that she was never able to walk properly again. Yet rather than letting this discourage her efforts to improve the lives of her beloved soldiers, she became even more convinced of the need for a permanent Soldiers' Home in Portsmouth.

Ports like Portsmouth groaned when troops returned from the never ending wars and skirmishes of the Victorian era. There was no patriotic welcome for the brave soldiers and sailors. For the servicemen would come armed with pockets full of wages, ready to squander it away in the many pubs, music halls and brothels long before they went home to their wives and families. If the soldier or sailor had served abroad for several years, his accumulated wages could be quite significant. They could have transformed his life. But the majority "would have their fling and spend their money, and lose health and character and their very souls," wrote Sarah, despairingly.

Sarah describes how "soldiers were drinking spirits out of pewter-pots, and almost forcing passers-by to partake; cabs were driving from one public-house to another loaded inside and out with drunken, shouting men and women".

Perhaps it was no wonder the town quaked with fear and trepidation. So it was a brave woman who tried to tackle the problem – one which the higher echelons of the army and navy did their best to ignore. But who was this Sarah Robinson? And what fuelled her desire to help soldiers and, in so doing, improve the environment of the ports and garrison towns?

We are fortunate that Sarah, like many of the other temperance reformers featured in this book, was an inveterate writer. She wrote articles, journals and three autobiographical books: *Yarns* (1892), *A Life Record* (1898) and *My Book* (1914). In the preface to the second book, Sarah said she didn't trust others to write a true account of her work and that she was going to destroy all her records so that no-one could attempt to do so. Yet, clearly she hadn't actually thrown her papers away by the time she wrote her final book in 1914. This time, she was writing "to please myself" rather than the publishers! It is easy to see how the self-deprecating humour, so evident in her writings, would have appealed to soldiers. Sarah was a natural raconteur.

Sarah's journals were like scrapbooks in which she made notes, wrote short poems and stuck in photographs and pictures. She embellished the books with drawings and colourful borders. I thought these had all been lost or, as Sarah had threatened, destroyed. To my great delight I have discovered that at least one survives – in the proud possession of a distant branch of Sarah's family now living in South Africa. It even includes an original letter to Sarah from Florence Nightingale.

Sarah described herself as "a queer child" and certainly when you read her account of how she spent her time, it is hard to disagree. Her father was a staunch Calvinist, her mother a remote delicate figure who died whilst Sarah was still young. She was happiest alone, roaming the countryside around her parents' estate, 'Heasmonds' in East Hoathly, Sussex. There Sarah 'saw about' things, rather than just read about them. This included all the processes of brewing in the estate's own brew-house, something Sarah simply accepted as the norm.

To the constant dismay of her nurses, Sarah was mischievous, though she calmed down under the influence of a cousin, Sarah Verrall, or 'dear old Coz' as she was affectionately called. But she was "never loving or lovable", a strange description for one who later gave so much of herself to care for others.

Sarah hated dolls but played with bows and arrows, knives and even guns, causing several injuries to her brothers in the process. She was fascinated by tales and poems about soldiers, revelling in their brave exploits. She admired "the gorgeous beings who stood sentry at the Pavilion" in Brighton.

In her books, Sarah makes fun of herself describing how a tramp came begging to their kitchen door. He called himself 'an old soldier' and spun a long tale of his misfortunes. Despite the misgivings of the kitchen staff, on Sarah's insistence he was given food, a few pence and two of her father's old shirts. Still Sarah didn't think this enough and ran after him to present him with a shilling of her own. But next morning, the landlady of the village pub arrived at the house with the two shirts. The tramp had sold them for beer. When the woman had seen Mr Robinson's name in the shirts, she thought perhaps they had been stolen. Poor Sarah was teased mercilessly about her 'old soldier' by her brothers.

As a child, Sarah disliked going to church, which she found very boring. The two hours of a "totally unintelligible" service each Sunday at the Jireh Chapel in Lewes were dreaded. However, it was the religious zeal of another soldier, visiting his sister in the village when home on leave, which restored Sarah's faith in the goodness of servicemen. The man had been converted whilst serving abroad and started to hold simple cottage meetings for prayer and Bible readings in his sister's home. No one could tease Sarah for being impressed by this soldier.

Sarah was happy wandering around the village of East Hoathly. She would often read the Bible to elderly cottagers. After her father built his own chapel on the estate, she and her sister would run an informal Sunday school there. Her father was not exactly encouraging, telling her, "When the blind lead the blind, both generally fall into the ditch." For, at this stage, Sarah was merely acting as the dutiful daughter of the squire, not out of any religious conviction of her own.

School in Brighton brought Sarah little pleasure but saw the start of her spinal problems. She would later blame long periods of sitting on benches with no backs to them for her disability. Whatever the root cause, that certainly can't have helped. Her father, recently widowed, had always been fixated about his own health. He now made it his mission to find a cure for his daughter. Poor Sarah endured years of torment – 15 months stretched flat on a couch; another year "pickled, pummelled, and plastered weekly". Her internal organs were so damaged that she was not expected to live for long. But the medics had not factored in Sarah's extraordinary steely will. They couldn't have imagined that, 40 years later, she would be embarking on gruelling fund-raising tours, covering over

1,000 miles, delivering speeches in 26 English cities.

Sarah decided to change her place of worship to Chiddingly Church, simply because the sermons there were shorter. Little did she know that it would be one of these sermons, delivered by the preacher Mr Vidal, which would change her perspective on religion and life. The 'call' was "unsought and unexpected" she recalled. She now started to study the Bible assiduously.

By chance, at this time, she was also trying to help a drunkard in the village. She used to go and fetch him out of the pub, take him home, give him some strong coffee and wait while his wife got him safely to bed. The next day she would "pray, weep and plead" with him. He'd promise to stay sober, then within the week he'd be back in the pub. It occurred to Sarah that she was being hypocritical, for she still enjoyed wine regularly with her meals. So she consulted the vicar, Mr Vidal. He was appalled at the idea that she should abstain. In his view such self sacrifice was quite unnecessary. Like many clergy, he obviously enjoyed a drink himself.

Even when, in 1857, she was based in London, undergoing treatment on her spine but continuing her charitable works, she continued to enjoy alcohol. As she later reflected, "I have often thought how strange it was that my stay in London did not make me a teetotaller, seeing misery enough through drink; but I did not come into contact with any teetotal fellow workers and do not remember thinking of the subject at all." Her experience reflects the fact that the teetotal movement had not really caught on in the south at this stage, despite having been a major force in the north of England for over 20 years.

Sarah was prepared to defy convention. She joined a Presbyterian Church but was subsequently banned from communion there. Her 'sin'? – organizing 'cottage meetings' and having the audacity, as a mere woman, to speak at them. She started visiting the sick in hospital but instead of quiet words, in sepulchred tones, she told stories to make the patients laugh. Her storytelling skills developed with practice. She later found her 'yarns' were much better received by soldiers than sophisticated lectures.

She also had to come to terms with her disability. When a doctor told her she mustn't marry or have a family, she was understandably distraught. She was only in her early twenties. The future must have looked bleak. But she prayed long and hard until she heard the answer she needed: "The unmarried woman careth for the things of the Lord".

In due course she was able to be quite philosophical about her condition, saying that perhaps it helped her focus on her work, "cutting me off from so many sources of enjoyment which might otherwise have engrossed my life". Her sense of humour probably helped hide what must have been considerable mental and physical anguish, the normal dreams of a young woman smashed to smithereens. So, on seeing the results of a family portraiture session, she wryly commented, "One does not fully know how 'plain' one is until this has been done."

Like many members of the landed gentry, Sarah's father hit financial problems, having invested unwisely. He decided to sell his sizable estate in East Hoathly, to ensure he had enough money to provide for each of his children on his death – a laudable intention but one which caused Sarah a great deal of distress. She had loved her childhood home. For a while the family lived in rented accommodation in Brighton, before making a permanent move to Guildford, Surrey.

Yet it was Guildford which was to provide Sarah with her first regular contact with soldiers, at the nearby Aldershot barracks. With the aid of Eddard the donkey, who drew her invalid chair through the streets, Sarah would visit soldiers who were billeted in local pubs, giving them books and simply talking to them as fellow human beings. She saw them as men who had risked their lives in the Crimean War or the Indian Mutiny, not, as many did, as the scum of the earth who terrorized the streets on drunken rampages. Of course, her friends and family thought her "really dreadful" for going to places they would not dream of venturing into.

She would also go out to talk to some of the hundreds of tramps who passed by their house each year. She discovered many were men of good education, some even former clergymen, all brought low by alcohol abuse. Once again, Sarah became conscious of her own drinking habits. However she tried to excuse it, she started to acknowledge that she was very dependent on a glass of wine "when overtired or sleepless, or suffering from neuralgia, as I frequently did".

Was it by design, or a happy coincidence, that some of the new friends she made in Guildford were teetotallers? Sarah was drawn to people like Miss Colebrook and her brother who had founded the first Band of Hope in Guildford. Soon she was running a school for older girls in a room above the brother's business premises.

It was a lecture entitled 'Stop the Leak' at Guildford's Newman Hall, in April 1861 which ultimately convinced Sarah that she should sign the pledge. But she allowed herself a let out clause – she'd give abstinence a two year trial. Her father was unsupportive, to say the least, even offering her £50 to break the pledge. When she became ill, Sarah's doctors also prescribed wine and stout, but she stuck to her resolution. She'd begun to realize she could do more work with drunkards if she wasn't one of those "little drop Christians" – one of her many wonderful digs at some of the hypocritical do-gooders she encountered.

Sarah's first visit to Aldershot barracks was in 1860, in the company of a small group of Scottish friends. She was shocked to learn just how unpopular soldiers were. When she was asked to pray for the 69th Regiment, then serving in Burma, Sarah took it upon herself to write regular letters to the regiment, developing a comradeship with the men which was to last many years.

Before long, Sarah was a regular visitor at the barracks. In 1863 she helped Mrs Louisa Daniell, the widow of an officer, set up an Institute and Mission Hall in Aldershot to provide an alcohol-free centre where soldiers could relax and also attend lectures and classes. This experience taught Sarah a lot, lessons she would later put to good use in Portsmouth. She had discovered her flair for organizing or, as she called it, "an infinite capacity for taking pains".

Despite Mrs Daniell not being a teetotaller, Sarah was eventually allowed to form a Total Abstinence Society at the Institute. By the end of the first year, it boasted 500 members. But her relationship with Mrs Daniell was at times strained. The widow didn't share Sarah's view that the soldiers should be treated as equals. Whilst Mrs Daniell was happy to remain aloof in her room upstairs, it was noted by an officer that "when anything queer is going on, you'll find Miss Robinson in the thick of it". When Mrs Daniell decided to pass the role of superintendent to a man, it was a clear snub to Sarah, who took the hint and returned home to Guildford.

Sarah's own account of her experiences in Aldershot perhaps explain why her activities caused concern to the more staid Mrs Daniell, who probably felt Sarah was in danger of bringing the institute into disrepute. On one occasion, whilst looking for a sick woman whom she was supposed to be visiting, Sarah inadvertently stumbled into what she described as "a thieves' kitchen". To her horror, Sarah was shut inside, a rough looking man guarding the door to prevent her escape. She must have been terrified but she kept her wits about her. She apologized for intruding and offered to sing to the gang, promising a song they would never have heard before. She then proceeded to sing a hymn. To her surprise, the stunned audience said she could come again. And so started regular visits where Sarah would tell Bible stories and sing hymns.

When Sarah left the Aldershot Institute, she had a farewell tea party with this motley crew. She took the provisions; they provided the 'tea service', which consisted "chiefly of old jam-pots, clothes pegs to stir with, publicans' *borrowed* beer cans to 'mash' the tea in, and pieces of newspaper for plates". Sarah clearly saw the absurdity of such situations. But she also believed she had converted at least four of the gang to more Godly ways.

Whilst many ladies pursuing philanthropic activities would have concentrated on the women and children, Sarah was the first to admit she didn't like babies. She dreaded mothers' meetings where their screeching offspring disrupted proceedings. The idea of a crèche, which she later operated at the Portsmouth Institute, was born. Over time, she developed a rapport with teenage boys, but only by resorting to teaching them military drills. But she did have a keen understanding of the plight of the wives and mothers of soldiers. She even gained a reputation for being "good at love letters" which she would write on behalf of illiterate men.

Sarah maintained her correspondence with the 69th regiment. When they returned to England in 1864, they were quartered at Gosport, on the west side of Portsmouth harbour. Sarah was invited down to a large tea party. To her dismay, she was seated, not with the men, but with the officers and ladies. Sarah hated small talk. The chairman of the meeting, somewhat reluctantly but because one of the speakers hadn't turned up, asked Sarah to say a few words "to the women". As Sarah described it – a few words sufficed for the women, then she went on directly to address her former correspondents "to their great delight". There was "great handshaking afterwards, which the officers and ladies kindly pretended not to see".

This meeting was followed by another, at which Sarah was the main speaker. But she'd started to make waves. Articles appeared in the local press. It seemed many people didn't appreciate her outspokenness and her criticism of the area – which she felt encouraged returning soldiers and sailors to drink and waste their hard earned money. Word spread to London. The military authorities decreed she was "subversive to military discipline". This must have hurt. Her intentions were the exact opposite. By promoting abstinence from alcohol, Sarah hoped to improve discipline. The formation of a regimental temperance society was banned; further meetings prohibited. By the time the 69th regiment moved on just a few months later, the men had squandered over £6,000 of their savings; 500 stripes and good-conduct badges had been lost "through drink and dissipation". And Sarah's frustrations with the authorities had only just begun.

For the next eight years, from 1865 to 1873, she would travel around the country, visiting barracks and setting up small groups. In *Yarns*, she wrote a wonderful description of herself at this time, "Imagine an ungraceful thickset young woman, buttoned up in a large waterproof cloak with its serviceable sleeves, cape and pockets; thick boots, skirts well off the ground, felt hat, and smooth dark hair. She is pale and ugly, but has earnest eyes that can look a man straight in the face without being stared or sneered down. She is armed with a large hand-bag containing Testaments, small books and bright cards – not forgetting a pocket pledge-book, and sweeties for the children." She paints a picture of a formidable lady, yet one who was also struggling to overcome her innate shyness.

In Brighton she secured a grant from the Naval and Military Bible Society to distribute Bibles and tracts, as she went to visit troops in their billets. But it was often the military chaplains who objected to Sarah's meetings. They clearly felt she was usurping their authority. Perhaps they also recognized that she was highlighting the need for work which they themselves should have been doing. On one occasion, when Sarah was speaking in a school-room, the chaplain had the poor school master arrested on the grounds that Sarah was not "an approved person". Sarah had to appeal directly to the Colonel to overrule the officious cleric. In a practical riposte, Sarah got herself registered as a lecturer, under the heading 'Military Education', in the Parliamentary Blue Book.

It was during this period that the nickname 'The Soldiers' Friend' was first given to Sarah. She proudly recorded in her memoirs how one soldier wrote "We call Miss Robinson by that name [The Soldiers' Friend] because she isn't like some people who try to do us good; she does not sit at the top of the stairs and tell us what we ought to do, but she comes down and takes us by the hand and looks us in the face, and leads us in the right way". Indeed so popular did Sarah become with the soldiers themselves that almost any lady who took an interest in the welfare of soldiers was likely to be addressed as 'Miss Robinson'.

For Sarah was much more at home with soldiers than with her peers. When journeying by train, she would deliberately seek out a carriage with soldiers in it – something most people would try to avoid. "Not that I *talked* much; what men like is a sympathetic and intelligent *listener*". In contrast, Sarah hated the "compliments and raptures" of fine ladies when she talked about her work at fashionable 'drawing-room meetings'. But this was to become a necessary evil to fund her work.

Sarah didn't work alone. She employed the services of a very large teapot – perhaps the most travelled teapot of its day. She found that soldiers responded well to the notion of a real tea party "with a white cloth, nice china, vase of flowers, thin bread and butter, and other dainties". Perhaps not surprisingly, as she travelled around, she discovered that at some of her lodgings soldiers were not welcome, even for tea with a respectable lady. So there would then be a pressing need to find a suitable location for the tea parties.

It was at one such tea party in Colchester in June 1871 that Sarah met Thomas Tufnell of The Queen's Bays, 2nd Dragoon Guards. Tufnell went on to become Sarah's faithful helper for the next 18 years, someone she trusted implicitly. In 1873, Sarah arranged for him to have two months' leave so he could accompany her when she set up her caravan and tents for the Dartmoor manoeuvres, but then the order was revoked. Unbeknown to Sarah, Tufnell purchased his discharge so as not to let Sarah down.

Sarah also built up a group of staunch female friends, such as Alice Burt (neé Halls) and Miss Grant who helped her in many of her enterprises. Each brought their own strengths. Miss Grant, for example, wouldn't venture into the barracks but she was excellent at the Bible readings and tea parties. She also helped Sarah at Chatham where they found lodgings in the home of the widow of a marine sergeant. Before they left, they had persuaded their landlady, to whom Sarah paid 5/- a week, to keep her kitchen open as a soldiers' prayer-room with coffee and cake provided. This small project grew into a Wesleyan Soldiers' Home. It was an example of how Sarah could sow seeds which she encouraged others to grow on.

Sarah did get some support for her work from the National Temperance League (NTL). After attending its annual meeting in 1867, she approached the NTL secretary for some financial help with her army work and was given a small supply of temperance literature. The following year after Sarah spoke at the NTL's Ladies Conference, *The Saturday Review*, an influential newspaper which claimed to represent educated opinion, published what Sarah describes as "a nasty article", *The Ladies on the Temperance Platform*. But however negative, publicity often helps a cause. The NTL was prompted into donating £10 worth of books for Sarah to distribute to soldiers and later gave her a further £20 towards the cost of tea meetings.

Most significantly, the NTL decided to make teetotalism in the army and navy a special feature of its next big meeting in London's Exeter Hall in 1869. Sarah took a group of 46 non-commissioned officers and old soldiers, representing 17 different regiments to the meeting. They were joined by some artillery from Woolwich and 60 lads from the training ship Warspite. This became an annual event; soldiers proud to display their teetotal credentials. The need for a culture change within the army, the navy, and society in general, was gradually being recognized.

In 1871, the teetotal muster-roll of the 46th regiment was proudly unfurled at the NTL's meeting, a great list of 250 names streaming down from the high platform to the floor. The dramatic gesture was designed to show that, with hard work, it was possible to change ingrained habits.

But it really was hard work and Sarah's health was not good. Many times she would collapse after meetings but she rarely rested. Diary entries, quoted in her autobiographies, understate her suffering. "Was ill in cab going home; suppose I must have fainted; fell down in a heap and smashed my best hat. Nobody with me."

Sarah had also become the main point of contact for any army family in distress. Mothers or wives would write to her asking that she check up on their loved ones, sometimes with pitiable tales of how the man had fallen back into his old drinking ways. Sarah found chasing backsliders emotionally and physically draining. In the 21st century we are used to mobile communications, but of course in Sarah's time all communication was by letter or word of mouth. Ultimately she was forced to take a pragmatic decision that she would only follow up people for three years, then they were on their own.

The NTL's support also added to Sarah's workload. She gave many lectures at their behest. She had to produce regular reports for publication in the NTL's *Temperance Journal*. The NTL encouraged her to visit women in Winchester Jail. Sarah found this a huge challenge until she decided to dismiss the warders and go in amongst the women, just talking in a soft voice. She started to visit the jail regularly. Later she would write that she felt a "great love" for the women and could easily have devoted herself to work amongst them, if she hadn't already devoted herself to working with soldiers.

It helped that Sarah got on well with the NTL committee. Major-General F Eardley-Wilmot, vice-president of the NTL, became one of her staunchest supporters. She enjoyed the committee's "straight business-like, purposeful questioning, so different to the silly questions ladies often ask". This comment undoubtedly reflects Sarah's frustrations at some of the ladies who attended fund-raising drawing-room meetings.

She may not have been a strident feminist, but Sarah did recognize and value women's role in the home and in wider society. A revealing comment in her journal says, "People always say *a woman is at the bottom of it* when anything bad befalls a man; they do not say, when a good thing happens, that *a woman is at the top of it*, but it is so all the same."

The NTL took on the job of providing a coffee room, with temperance literature, in every regiment where the commanding officer sanctioned it. The UK Band of Hope also helped Sarah establish the Army Band of Hope. Whenever a regimental temperance society opened, a Band of Hope for the children was formed. Not only did this help the younger generation but it often gave employment to retired teetotal soldiers.

At the NTL's request, Sarah wrote a small book *Christianity and Teetotalism, a Voice from the Army*, with extracts from 64 soldiers' letters. This was also a response to what she and others perceived as attacks on her work by the Plymouth Brethren. The Brethren believed women should play a silent, supportive role in worship; that evangelism should be led by men. So conflict with Sarah was inevitable.

Although Sarah never sought personal gifts or praise, one of her most treasured possessions was a patchwork rug made up of over 28,000 octagons, each no bigger than the old sixpence, all hand-stitched by a soldier, Private Roberts of the 17th Regiment. Private Roberts had been a great drinker, who feared he could easily be tempted back into his old habits through want of something to do. But a friend of Sarah's, Rev. Hardy suggested the soldier take up patchwork to keep himself occupied. Some 15 months later, the rug was complete. The Reverend showed it to General Sir Hope Grant who promptly bought it for £10 on behalf of the NTL Committee, who then presented it to Sarah. She admitted to "a thrill of gratified vanity" when publically praised, instantly followed by "keen self-contempt. What fools we be!"

It was under the NTL banner that Sarah went, in 1873, to Dartmoor and Cannock Chase to join the militia on autumn manoeuvres. The militia was a volunteer citizen force (the forerunner of the Territorial Army) with rifle, artillery and engineering corps. As well as annual local camps, every two or three years there would be brigade manoeuvres, with the militia training alongside regular artillery and cavalry. Such "sham-fighting" exercises would see 10,000 soldiers in harsh conditions and no creature comforts; no recreation or refreshment except in big canteen tents set up by local enterprising brewers. Sarah hatched a plan to compete with the brewers but she needed permission from the military authorities. She also needed money and people. Through the support of Sir Hope Grant, Sarah got her approval; the NTL agreed to cover expenses but only on condition that Sarah herself led the enterprise – quite a big demand for a woman already severely handicapped by her spinal condition.

But Sarah didn't hesitate, despite the constant rain, a leaking caravan and an exhausting schedule. When, at times, she was too ill to surface from her caravan, she would simply hold meetings through the window, issuing instructions and providing words of comfort where required. She even managed to retain her unique sense of humour, recalling in her journal how during one service the benches would sink into the peaty ground, "Men are seen with their heels in the air and their heads in the mud, NOT an edifying spectacle."

If she saw a real need, Sarah would rarely take no for an answer. During manoeuvres, the men had no means of sending money home to their families. The Post Office refused to open a Camp Post Office, then refused Sarah permission to operate one herself. So she went ahead anyway, despite the threat of prosecution. "I had to risk that; it did not trouble my conscience at all."

From the soldiers themselves, Sarah received nothing but kindness and appreciation. She loved the way the NTL banner was interpreted as "New Tea Lounge", "Never Touch Liquor" or, best of all, "Never Too Late". But she had little time for the tourists who found their way up to the temporary camp, expecting to partake of free refreshment and hurling insults when refused. Thankfully, there were other more distinguished and influential visitors. Stories of the work began to appear in the press.

Even so, when she moved her caravan, tents and team on to Cannock Chase where other regiments were on manouevres, she had to do battle with the General before she could get her marquees inside the camp. He had been petitioned by the local brewers and, to appease them, he demanded the removal of the NTL flagstaff and the very flag Sarah had spent 13 hours laboriously mending. She must have felt very irritated but, as she reported to the NTL, there had been "no time for speeches or organizing meetings. 'Deeds, not words,' was our motto." Yet those deeds had been effective. A huge amount of temperance literature was handed out and 140 soldiers took the pledge.

The publicity and the obvious success of the Dartmoor and Cannock Chase enterprises would help Sarah with her next endeavour – the project she had been quietly leading towards – a Soldiers' Institute in Portsmouth. She had identified the need and gradually realized that unless she took steps to address it, no-one else was going to do so. There had once been a small Soldiers' Home in the town, thanks to the efforts of the Rev. Carus-Wilson from the Isle of Wight who came over once a month to visit soldiers at Portsmouth. In 1861 the War Office had even commissioned a report which highlighted the need for a bigger and better Soldiers' Home, but nothing was done.

By 1872, Sarah was actively campaigning for an Institute in the town. A friend had introduced her to Ellice Hopkins, a writer who later became known as a social purity campaigner. Ellice was deeply impressed by Sarah's dedication. She wrote a short book *Active Service* to raise money for the Portsmouth Institute and was one of the provisional committee who helped steer the project forward.

Two other key supporters, and fellow committee members, were Sir Arthur J. Lawrence and Major-General G.F. Eardley-Wilmot. The latter wrote an impassioned letter to *The Times* in April 1872, publicizing the book and Sarah's plans and asking well-wishers of the army to help. Interestingly he states that Miss Robinson herself was willing to manage the Institute for "1 year, or more if necessary". Clearly at this stage Sarah had hoped to be able to hand over the project to others once it was well-established but some 20 years later she was still there. And even after she retired to the New Forest, she was drawn back to take over again as Honorary Superintendent in 1898.

In her fund-raising work, Sarah painted a colourful scene of the squalor and drinking culture of Portsmouth and the troops who passed through it. Such outspokenness didn't endear her to the civic authorities. Looking back on her life in 1939 *The Portsmouth Evening News* called her "The Best Hated Woman in Portsmouth." This title sums up Sarah well. She refused to be browbeaten by her detractors; she wouldn't compromise her principles.

As money started to come in, Sarah met with the Vicar of Portsmouth and the military chaplain, Archdeacon Wright. She expected their support. Instead she found organized opposition. Archdeacon Wright was to prove a thorn in Sarah's side for many years. His main objection seemed to be to the provision of Bible-reading classes in the proposed Institute. Of course, he claimed, he supported improved facilities for the men. He could even, grudgingly, support the principle of temperance teaching. But he would not tolerate others teaching God's word to the troops. Clearly he thought this role was his, and only his. So he craftily offered his backing, including help with fund-raising, if Sarah dropped the religious element of her plans.

Sarah was adamant. "I could do nothing without the Bible," she protested. But she referred the matter to her committee, whilst making it clear she would personally withdraw from the project if they decided to go ahead without incorporating religious instruction as an integral part of the Institute's work. The Committee backed her and the search for a suitable site proceeded.

The War Office was approached and Sarah was delighted when she heard a grant of land was being made, on the understanding that the government had no further responsibility, financial or managerial, for it. The enterprising Sarah still managed to extract a promise of stone from old fortifications which were being demolished and the use of labour, though not free, from the Royal Engineers. But Archdeacon Wright, and some other local people, including brewers, weren't happy. Unpleasant meetings followed but Sarah continued with her plans. Then the Archdeacon lobbied the Duke of Cambridge when he was visiting troops in the town. Suddenly a condition was imposed on the government's grant of the site – no Bible work should be introduced there.

Once more, Sarah stuck to her principles and her committee backed her. The Institute was "to be a house for God or I wish to have nothing to do with it," she thundered. So the government's site was relinquished. This may have seemed a foolish move but actually Sarah had another site in mind, the old Fountain Inn in the High Street, notorious as the location of a lethal boxing match. However, the local fund-raising committee resigned, claiming the ambitious plans were now too big.

"Probably if I had waited till all our well-wishers were agreed as to *where* and *how* the Institute should be established we should never have got one at all," Sarah wrote. She put down the necessary £100 deposit to secure The Fountain and sent her trusted right-hand man Thomas Tufnell and his family to take up residence there. By January 1874 Sarah herself was living there. Although she'd spent much of the previous eight years travelling and working around the country, she had always been able to retreat home to her father's house at Guildford. Now she secured from him a regular allowance and moved out permanently.

Nine months later, the Institute was formally opened by General Sir Hope Grant. Poor Sarah was so ill that on the big day she was unable to participate in the proceedings. An illuminated address from 200 non-commissioned officers was handed to Sir Arthur Lawrence to pass on her. Sarah might perhaps have been disappointed that so few staff or officers of the garrison attended (Sarah blamed the influence of Archdeacon Wright) but the rank and file soldiers came in their hundreds.

The Institute proved a huge success from the outset. The Archdeacon's continued opposition only served to create publicity. Sarah actually reckoned it brought in several thousand pounds of funding. At one stage, the Archdeacon persuaded the Catholic chaplain to join him in attacking the Institute, on the false premise that Catholics were not welcome there. But the Catholics soon realized that the hospitality of the Institute was open to all denominations.

Local brewers and publicans also fiercely opposed the project. Whenever a troop-ship arrived in dock, Sarah would go aboard, handing out literature about the Institute and the facilities it offered. This meant passing through "a mob of landsharks and women who cursed me ... mud was thrown into my cab, our windows were broken, doormats cut up, disgusting anonymous letters sent ..."

Sobriquets such as "Mars-smitten Old Maid" (Mars being the god of war) and "Oratorial Gladiator" amused rather than hurt Sarah on a personal level. But the adverse publicity did initially put many women off coming to work at the Institute and Sarah desperately needed help. By October 1876 she had just three permanent, trustworthy female helpers. Many others came and went, their foolish romantic notions of the work soon dashed by the sheer physical effort involved.

It wasn't the soldiers' glory which impressed or inspired Sarah. It was what she called "his sadness – the isolation, contempt, unkindness and cruel temptations of his lot," which brought out the "motherliness" in her. Soldiers were her surrogate family.

The fundraising had to continue unabated, alongside the actual running of the Institute. Sarah found practical and innovative ways to develop the project. The double-flight of railed stone steps at the front of the old Fountain Inn was a notorious pick-up point for local prostitutes. So Sarah had new steps made inside the front door, demolished the old steps and even persuaded the local authority to pay her £15 for relinquishing such a large piece of the pavement. She had the words 'Soldiers' Institute' painted in white letters six foot high on the sloping roof, so it could be seen by soldiers leaving and arriving at the port. Clearly, Sarah didn't intend to keep a low profile.

Archdeacon Wright continued his opposition but when he claimed to be complaining on behalf of General Sir Hastings Doyle, Sarah called his bluff. She contacted the General directly and he

Portrait of Ann Carlile – founder of The Band of Hope
by kind permission of the Trustees of Lambeth Palace Library

Sarah Robinson at 70 – The Soldiers' Friend
from *My Book* by Sarah Robinson 1914

Sarah as a young woman,
the NTL wagon on Dartmoor
and The Soldiers' Institute
Portsmouth
all from *My Book* by Sarah
Robinson 1914

Sarah's Invalid Coach leaving the Institute for a
gruelling speaking tour of England
from *My Book* 1914

The Officers' House, Portsmouth
from *Yarns* by Sarah Robinson 1892

Agnes Weston
from *My Life among the Blue-Jackets* 1909

The Royal Sailors Rest, Devonport and The Royal
Sailors Rest, Portsmouth
from *My Life among the Blue-Jackets* by Agnes Weston 1909

Agnes Weston and Sophia Wintz welcoming the Japanese Navy
from *My Life among the Blue-Jackets* by Agnes Weston 1909

Agnes Weston at a Royal Navy Temperance Society meeting
from *My Life among the Blue-Jackets* by Agnes Weston 1909

Agnes Weston's funeral in 1918, with full naval honours
from a postcard kindly loaned by Graham Brooks

confirmed his support for her work at the Institute. Moreover she told the Archdeacon she would only stop her Sunday school when there was one established in the garrison. She effectively shamed him into action. "The poor Archdeacon!" she wrote. "He has to work now to keep up with us; he has two Sunday Schools in barracks, and is giving the children a Tea and new prayer-books. He visits … as never before, and has commenced a men's Bible-class."

Worse was to come for the Archdeacon – he was passed over for the post of Chaplain-General; the position going to a civilian. He became very bitter. Both he and Sarah realized his persistent opposition to her work had harmed his chances of promotion. But when he left Portsmouth in December 1876, Sarah could not help commenting, "I am really rather sorry, as his perpetually running about telling people *not* to visit us was a continual advertisement, and brought many out of curiosity."

One building was never going to be enough for Sarah's ambitious plans. Before long she had acquired the adjacent properties and transformed the former stables and tap room into a lecture hall.

A contemporary account of the Institute appears in *Yacht Voyage Round England*, written in 1879 by WHG Kingston. Harry was a lucky young man who travelled around the coast of Britain with his father, a retired Navy Captain, during an extended summer school holiday. His description of the Soldiers' Institute might owe something to promotional literature Harry picked up in the town, but it is quite fulsome.

"At the entrance are rooms where the soldiers and sailors can see their friends, and then there is a large bar, where, although no intoxicating drinks can be obtained, tea, coffee and beverages of all sorts are served. Near it is a large coffee room. Passing through the house, we entered a very nice garden, on the right of which is a bowling-green and a skittle-alley; and we then came to a very handsome hall which serves for religious meetings, lectures, concerts, teas and other social gatherings. There were also rooms in which the men can fence or box. A large reading-room (with a good library) and Bible-classroom are on the second floor; and at the top of the house are dormitories, making up a considerable number of beds for soldiers, as also for their wives and families, who may be passing through Portsmouth either to embark or have come from abroad. There is a sewing-room for the employment of the soldiers' wives. A Children's Band of Hope meets every week. There is even a smoking-room for the men, and hot and cold baths. Indeed, a more perfect place for the soldier can nowhere be found ..."

Sarah used the Institute as a hub from which to expand her operations at Portsmouth. She soon realized that she couldn't hand over the enterprise to others and turn away – not while there was work to be done. It was in her nature to identify a problem and then swiftly identify a solution. Finding the money to put her plans into practice sometimes took a little longer. She was constantly lecturing and writing. She wrote a special book for departing troops, *Good-bye*, later adding a further seven volumes to the series. A generous friend paid to have 100,000 copies printed.

Sarah also became concerned about the welfare of the women and children on board the troopships. She started to collect and distribute clothing and blankets to them. She noticed how, at disembarkation, the troops would suffer long delays waiting on the jetty in the cold and wet, with no shelter, seats or food, until their onward transport was available. So, just as in her Dartmoor days, Sarah set up a cart on the jetty selling hot coffee, tea and buns to the men, dispensing the same to women and children for free. "Whatever the weather was I remained among the people until they were sent off." Eventually the Admiralty allowed her to erect a proper coffee-shed, and later even a waiting room, on the jetty.

In July 1876, tragedy struck the port with a massive explosion aboard HMS Thunderer. There were many fatalities and the hospital was packed with the severely injured. Sarah spent hours there reading, singing and talking. She also took it upon herself to visit the bereaved families. When members of the Enquiry Committee came down to Portsmouth, she provided hospitality at the Institute, where they "liked everything very much except the teetotalism".

Accommodation was always a problem. She rented various houses in Portsmouth and then sub-let them to soldiers' families. For, if soldiers had married without official permission, their wives would not be admitted to the barracks. She realised that the presence of officers in the main Institute was not always 'convenient', so she bought up the hotel next to the Lecture Hall, and later three adjoining houses, to provide a special house for officers.

Nor did she ignore the needs of young sailor-boys. On Sundays and Thursdays, the lads from the training ship St Vincent would swarm over the Institute. Their noise and exuberance meant many soldiers stayed away. So at the bottom of the Institute's garden, she had erected a two-storey building. The ground floor was used as a kitchen and baggage-store; the upper floor as a special room for the sailor-boys with a piano, games and books, and a telescope on the roof. Sarah was grateful that a young woman, Miss Rose, volunteered to take charge of this area of work.

Sarah even helped found a small Institute at Newport, on the Isle of Wight. This soon became independent of the Portsmouth operations, with two of Sarah's trusted helpers going over to run it.

In June 1879, Sarah received a letter from her heroine, Florence Nightingale, full of praise for her efforts: "…how glorious has been the work that you have accomplished." Sarah clearly treasured this letter. It was preserved, complete with envelope, a photograph of Miss Nightingale herself, and a scrap of a remembrance card, in her journal, with Sarah's own comment "…my heart was full of almost adoring reverence for her [Florence Nightingale] during the Crimean War; little as I imagined that she would be one of the first to encourage me when I was at last able to do something for the soldiers she had never ceased to love."

Of course it wasn't just soldiers who passed through Portsmouth. It was a big naval base and Sarah was acutely aware that sailors too had need of an Institute or Home. But, "though I wanted something *done*, I did not want *to do it*," Sarah wrote. She hoped, as did some of her high ranking friends in the Navy, that Agnes Weston, 'the Sailors' Friend' who had established an impressive Sailors' Rest at Devonport, near Plymouth, would start a similar project in Portsmouth. Sarah had first met Miss Weston at an NTL event in 1873. "I like her much", had been Sarah's verdict. But, at that stage, 1878, Miss Weston felt unable to help as there were still huge debts to pay off at Devonport.

As usual, Sarah couldn't sit back and see a need unmet. Initially she helped set up a small place in Camden Alley, working with an old seaman's missionary, Mr Blackah. But she soon felt this place was "worse than useless". With just 36 beds there were often fights between those who got in and those who didn't.

So she left Mr Blackah to run this place himself and bought a shop and several large warehouses in Queen Street, Portslea, to become a Sailors' Welcome. By 1880, it provided 250 beds, lockers, a large refreshment room, class room, reading room, baths and W.C.s, kitchens and stores – another very significant undertaking. In 1887, Queen Victoria's golden jubilee year, over 56,000 beds were let there.

By 1882, following another naval tragedy, Agnes Weston had started up her own Sailors' Rest at Landport, Portsmouth. Sarah was impressed. "For size, grandeur, and, I may say, usefulness, it beats mine all to fits," she declared. But she acknowledged that both schemes were needed. Sarah persuaded Agnes, with whom she appears to have been quite friendly, to take over some of her work with the sailor-boys and the sailors' wives. But she couldn't persuade Miss Weston to take on the Sailors' Welcome, in addition to her own Rest.

Sarah felt it necessary to ensure she kept the funding and expenses of her work with sailors quite separate from her work with soldiers. To establish the Sailors' Welcome, she put in money of her own and borrowed some on a mortgage. She maintained full personal financial responsibility for the Welcome until she retired, when the mortgagees took it over and leased it to Mr Pither, who had worked as Sarah's manager there.

She also set up a Mission Room at Eastney. After several years she found people to develop this and build a small hall, which they ran themselves. Later, Agnes Weston took over responsibility for this.

One of Sarah's earliest projects was a simple coffee-house and mission room on the Camber, an area full of fishermen and 'waterside' people, at the time a very squalid place. This wasn't a facility for soldiers or sailors but for the locals, who, perhaps jealous of the facilities in the Institute, lobbied Sarah for a place of their own. But as the neighbourhood improved, Sarah was able to close this down.

For by 1883, it had been superseded by another project – the Blue Ribbon coffee tavern and mission hall in Nobbs Lane. This was a notorious district. There was a pub, The Sir John Falstaff, and two courts of dreadful housing. "I have seen and heard things [there] in broad daylight too shamelessly disgusting to print," declared Sarah. But the police weren't interested. If she didn't go there, then she wouldn't get so annoyed about it, was their response.

Sarah's response, typically, was to purchase the pub and the courts of houses and turn them into her coffee tavern and mission hall, which she opened in February 1883. This meant another £500 of her own money and a great deal of work fund-raising for the rest. But ultimately the people of the district had their centre – a place of their own, somewhere for them as the Institute was for soldiers. Sarah called this "a most useful and happy branch of Institute work" for the soldiers themselves gave time, prayers and money to it. Many people gave up drink; many found God. "Homes were transformed, and a happy change was evident throughout the whole district." When Sarah retired the Salvation Army bought the premises and ran it for their 'rescue and social work'.

In 1879 and 1880, as men from the 21st Fusiliers were being sent out to fight in the Zulu War, many sent their families to Portsmouth "to be under Miss Robinson's wing till we come back". Their confidence was rewarded. Sarah found all the women decent lodgings in the town. She encouraged soldiers' wives to sew and the Institute paid for 5,000 pieces of their needlework.

Late 1880 saw the 1st Boer War and yet more departing troops. It also brought Emile, Lady Milbanke to the Institute as a worker. Sarah was delighted. Emile "supplied the very element that had been lacking ... a lady to represent the Institute among those of the Upper Circle in the Garrison – to call on officers' wives, dine at Government House, interview distinguished visitors, attend functions ..." – in other words, all the aspects of the work which Sarah herself hated so much. This aristocratic lady, whose brother had been a serving officer, was in practice "a very humble, loveable Christian" but even Sarah could appreciate how "her brougham and servants" impressed the powers-that-be in Portsmouth.

The sheer scale of Sarah's work was impressive. She was so incapacitated by back pain that she barely left the Institute between 1881 and 1889 and yet she still achieved huge growth in her various enterprises. If she couldn't get to meetings, the meetings came to her, as records from the YMCA in Portsmouth show.

To mark her 50th birthday, in 1884, Sarah formed the Society of

Little Friends of Soldiers and Sailors, recruited primarily from the families of her supporters. The children were encouraged to 'adopt' soldiers and write letters to them.

Still she felt the call, albeit reluctantly, to do more – in Alexandria, Egypt where British troops were now fighting. "It was a terrible thing when, early in 1884, the idea that I should have to provide [an Institute in Alexandria] took possession of me." But tales of sin and suffering at Alexandria found their mark in Sarah's heart. She sent Tufnell out to reconnoitre. Seeing at first hand the ruined property, the dirty drinking dens and the rife prostitution, he sent a telegram to Sarah, "Must have Institute." She simply replied "Go ahead" – a directive easier said than done. But Tufnell did find a site at a cost of £2,630, all of which had to be found within three months, together with the appropriate 'consideration' or bribe for a licence to build there. He then returned to England so he and Sarah could plan phase two.

They didn't waste any time. By September, Tufnell was again bound for Alexandria, this time taking out with him two workmen and the old iron Brompton Oratory, which Sarah had purchased for £750, plus fittings. This building was being dismantled to make way for a new grand church on the South Kensington site but, for Sarah's purposes, it was ideal. They were given free passage on board the ship Dunluce – a sign the authorities were delighted to have Sarah taking on responsibility for providing suitable facilities for their soldiers in Egypt. The Army allowed Woolwich Arsenal to be used as storage for items awaiting shipment to Alexandria; they provided free transport. The Duke of Cambridge even provided Tufnell with a letter of recommendation to General Sir Frederick Stephenson, commander of forces in Egypt. Sarah was amused by the Duke's remark, "Miss Robinson likes to have very big places," for the initial iron building was to be followed by a substantial stone house alongside.

A fatal accident, the sacrifice of a live lamb, over £12,000 and a lot of hard work later, the Institute was finally ready. It proved a huge hit with soldiers and sailors, and their families, stationed in Alexandria, as well as with British and American men working in banks and offices there. Florence Nightingale wrote to Sarah, praising her endeavours. "You always come in to do the work so needed."

This was work done at huge personal cost. Sarah had to sell her own possessions and borrow as much as she could in order for the scheme to go ahead. In time, she managed to raise enough to get her own money back but this meant a punishing schedule of talks and visits and her health was deteriorating every day. She placed adverts in *The Times* on a regular basis. By 18th March 1885, the Times advert stated that just £3,000 was needed to complete the payments on the Alexandria Institute, then it would be self-supporting. Sarah was punctilious in ensuring no funding intended for the Portsmouth enterprises was diverted to Egypt.

On 25th May 1885, *The Times* published a letter from Sarah together with a letter she had received from Colonel Baker VC Deputy Inspector-General of Gendarmerie and Police in Alexandria. In the first three months of its opening, the Institute had become "in the opinion of all the British community in Alexandria … a highly prized necessary of social life to us all". He wrote of its "influence for good", which, in his official capacity, he had noted – no doubt with some relief.

Tufnell could not be spared forever. Sarah needed his support back home. So a Reverend Lawrence and his wife became resident superintendents of the Alexandria Institute in 1886 and stayed there for many years.

Despite the diversion of the Alexandria Institute, Sarah hadn't finished extending her operations in Portsmouth. She had wanted, for a long time, to have a coffee shop in the Landport area. When the War Office started selling off Cambridge House and grounds, near the city's railway station, Sarah managed to acquire a significant section of the site, on which she built The Speedwell. By August 1890 this complex included both a 'Coffee Palace' and a Gospel Hall.

To fund the project, Sarah had pushed herself to the limit. Necessity being the mother of invention, she had come up with a solution, of sorts, to her need to travel – an ambulance-coach, specially designed and built for her, with a spring-bed and rubber-tyres. So June 1889 saw her embark on a gruelling three month fund-raising trip around England. *The Hampshire Telegraph* reported, in September 1889, how she was welcomed home by large crowds. Notwithstanding her exhaustion, she entertained them with tales of her adventures on her travels, "often provoking laughter". She was still the raconteur. She later wrote an account, *A Thousand Miles in an Invalid's Coach*.

On her travels she met fellow temperance luminaries such as Julia Wightman and Lady Henry Somerset. Two years later she was back on the road, this time travelling the length and breadth of Scotland, always preaching and always collecting money for her work.

Perhaps The Speedwell was the straw which broke the camel's back. For in her book *A Life Record* Sarah said she had made two great mistakes: the first, undertaking The Speedwell at all, the second passing it over to other hands in 1892. It wasn't so much the operation of the place, it was its need for funds, having been acquired and built with two mortgages each of £30,000. There was also the small matter of her own health. She was physically and mentally exhausted. She felt she had lost her grip on things, her "nerves irritable, memory and judgment failing".

Sarah most certainly could have done without old problems raising their heads again. Suddenly army chaplains were objecting to meetings in barracks, just as they had done over 20 years before. This time the dispute even got an airing in the House of Lords. Permission was reinstated, with the proviso that such meetings must be non-sectarian. Despite all the good work she was doing, an effigy of Sarah was paraded and burnt on bonfire night in Portsmouth. This insult must have hurt but Sarah found the strength to rise above it.

Before the end of 1891, Sarah had offered her resignation to the board of trustees which governed the Institute and they were actively seeking her successor. The trustees decided The Speedwell should be sold, to be carried on as a commercial enterprise. Sarah lost money financially. She accepted that the place provided "a most excellent temperance and commercial hotel, with splendid public restaurant". But she admits she wasn't perhaps as grateful as she might have been to be relieved of the pressure of this work. Under the new regime, the gospel work didn't continue, so Sarah felt obliged to set up a new Welcome Mission nearby, the expenses of which she met herself until the end of 1894.

In the autumn of 1892, Rev. JG Gregson, a former Portsmouth pastor who had been out to India and set up the Indian Temperance Association, arrived to take over the Soldiers' Institute. Initially Sarah had thought she would remain there, but soon "we learned how great a mistake it is for old workers to stay on under a new regime", despite everyone's best intentions.

Sarah didn't find letting go of her life's work easy. But she had loyal friends and a new home, The Hut in Burley in the New Forest. Sarah had designed The Hut herself, with her usual meticulous attention to detail. Still, old habits die hard. A small annexe, initially intended for her coach, soon became a Mission Hall. Miss Alice Walker, who had worked with Sarah for many years, lived with her and whenever she went away, another of the old 'Institute ladies' came in her place. Sarah used the time to complete *A Life Record*, a more complete autobiography than her earlier volume, *Yarns*.

Rev. Gregson only stayed at the Institute for two years, before returning to India. A friend of his, Sidney Smith, took over but in 1898 he resigned, on health grounds. In a postscript to *A Life Record*, Sarah says she felt the need to return and to re-establish "the old home-like rule of ladies". Clearly male management failed to provide the maternal touch she believed the soldiers needed. Yet in *My Book*, written in 1914, Sarah paid tribute to Sidney Smith. He'd done "his valiant best, without salary, in a whole-hearted, unselfish way".

Nonetheless, Sarah was appalled at the state of the place when she returned. She soon discovered the manageress was an "inveterate drunkard" who had obtained the position with false references. Although her services were promptly dispensed with, Sarah ensured the woman was found a supportive home. By Easter 1899, Alice Walker had assumed the role of Honorary Acting Superintendent and Sarah returned to Burley to write copious letters, edit a new magazine, *Ready,* and create a new garden, rediscovering "the old delight of planning things for myself" and using the unskilled labour of "men who would do exactly as they were told". Clearly Sarah had also rediscovered her sense of humour.

On her 70th birthday, Sarah issued a small book of choice text for each day of the year. This *Little Keepsake* became a treasured item for many soldiers, especially as she was persuaded to include in it a photograph of herself.

The trustees, in whom the ownership of the Institute and its satellite activities was vested, would meet regularly at The Hut. They recognized that Sarah was still such a pivotal figure that it would need not just a new Superintendent but another organization to replace her. They decided that, on Sarah's death, the Soldiers' Christian Association would be asked to take over the Institute. But by 1911, this transfer had begun to take place, "without waiting for the uncertain date of my death," Sarah wryly commented. Given the fact that she lived for another 10 years, this was perhaps a wise decision.

Throughout her working life, Sarah remained true to her belief that teetotalism could help bring a man to faith. "No longer blunted by drink, the man's conscience has fair play, and his mind is clear to receive words whereby he might be saved," she wrote. She was forever grateful to have had the opportunity to see the truth of these words in action.

By the time of Sarah's death in 1921, the soldier's lot had much improved. Her obituary in *The Hampshire Telegraph* on the 2nd December 1921 described her as "somewhat imperious, but with a heart of gold".

As Lord Wolseley wrote, "She never neglected her duty, and we soldiers know what a virtue that means in the best of us." British soldiers around the world had cause to be grateful for Sarah's warmth, generosity and dogged determination. She gave them an alternative to their drinking culture and she did so with a smile on her face, despite her own constant, crippling pain.

When we think of the Victorian era, the heroic efforts of Florence Nightingale in the Crimean War spring to mind. We might have heard of Mary Seacole, the Creole woman who went out to the front at her own expense and started up a hotel to accommodate and cater for injured troops. Both these women were admirers of Sarah's work. So, why has history today forgotten about Miss Robinson, the Soldiers' Friend? She overcame the prejudices of the military authorities to improve facilities for soldiers. She demonstrated what could be achieved by a determined woman in a man's world. And she didn't let her own physical disabilities stop her from doing what she felt needed to be done.

CHAPTER 7

Dame Agnes Weston (1840 – 1918) 'The Sailors' Friend'

Never before had a funeral with full naval honours been afforded to a female, but Agnes Weston was truly a woman who broke the mould. In October 1918, almost 2,000 officers and sailors joined Vice-Admiral Sir GF Thursby, Commander-in-Chief, representing the King, and Rear-Admiral Sir AJ Henniker-Hughan, the Admiral Superintendent, to say good-bye to their beloved "Aggie". Alongside them stood representatives from the Royal Marines, the Army, the Royal Air Force, the WRNS and the American Navy, together with Miss Sophia Wintz who had been Agnes's life-long friend and fellow-worker. After the service in the Dockyard Church at Devonport, the coffin was placed on a gun carriage and covered with the Union Jack. People lined the streets to pay their respects to 'The Sailors' Friend' as the carriage was drawn to the cemetery by sailors.

Admiral Beresford summed up the mood of the sailors when he wrote in *The Times*, "The lower deck of the British Navy has suffered an irreparable loss by the death of Miss Agnes Weston. It is impossible to overrate the self-sacrificing, unselfish, and chivalrous work that she undertook ... to benefit the men of the Fleet."

Indeed, just a few months before her death, Agnes had been made a Dame, awarded the GBE in the birthday honours list. British sailors throughout the world were thrilled by this recognition. They called it the "God Bless 'Er" medal. The story behind the award makes fascinating reading.

Agnes was born in 1840, to prosperous parents – her father being a barrister. Agnes may not have faced pressure to marry or find paid employment but a life of leisure and luxury was never for her. For the sake of her mother's health, the family moved from London to Bath and it was here that Agnes grew up into a talented young woman, deeply committed to Christian beliefs and to helping others less fortunate than herself.

She admitted to an adolescent wobble in her convictions, when a new clergyman, the Rev. James Fleming, took over the parish. She also struggled to resolve seeming conflicts between religion and science, especially astrology, an interest she shared with her father. But the patience and understanding of her parents and of the Rev. Fleming paid off. Perhaps they knew Agnes better than she knew herself at that stage. They certainly seem to have realized she had the passion and energy to devote her life to some 'calling' – what and when, or indeed how far-reaching that would be, no-one could have foreseen.

Agnes had a deep love of singing and music and, unusually for a female, went to study the organ at Gloucester cathedral, having been taught to play by her uncle. Years later she would still be putting these skills to good use, although perhaps not quite in the way her patron and tutor, Dr Wesley, had envisaged. But entertaining sailors by playing the harmonium at the Rests she herself had established proved, for Agnes, as rewarding as any cathedral recital.

Like many a young woman of her day, she became involved in teaching Sunday School. Unusually, though, Agnes developed a liking for teaching the 'difficult' boys. "I liked the unmanageable very much," she wrote in her memoirs, *My Life Among the Blue-Jackets*. She also started visiting patients at Bath United Hospital, taking flowers and fruit from the family's gardens. Soon she was giving a short gospel address on each ward every week. It was from the patients that Agnes learned of the work of Catherine Marsh, whose philanthropic efforts included trying to improve living conditions for sailors. In later life, the two women would correspond with each other, though there is no evidence that they ever met. But, in the wards of Bath hospital, a seed had been sown.

Agnes also started writing little booklets and religious tracts for various publishers – the start of a prolific literary output which would continue throughout her life.

As the 'unmanageables' grew up, Agnes found there was still a need for classes, somewhere where the men could bring their wives. Her father was very supportive of her endeavours and rented a Mission Hall to accommodate all the classes she was now running. Like many temperance workers, she was trying to create a social alternative, "a public-house without the drink". Yet at this stage, Agnes would still enjoy the occasional alcoholic drink herself.

When the Somerset Militia was training in the Bath area, Agnes was asked to help provide some recreational facilities. Whilst the officers were well provided for, the men themselves were often billeted in pubs – not the ideal training ground. Agnes found a disused shop which she fitted out as a coffee bar. Her sister, Emily, helped out. Together, Agnes and Emily raised funds to provide games, newspapers and books in a quiet writing room. Agnes would play the harmonium and encourage hymn singing. As the militia disbanded, many of the men went into the regular army. It was no wonder they realized how much they would miss the friendship and warmth of that first coffee bar.

Encouraged by the Society for the Welfare of the Soldier, Agnes wrote to some of the men, especially those who were practicing Christians. But fate was to intervene. For Agnes's calling was to be the welfare of sailors, the blue-jackets, rather than soldiers. It was one of her soldier correspondents who showed his letter to a sick-berth attendant, George Brown, on board HMS Crocodile. "Would this kind lady write to me?" enquired George. The answer was a definite "Yes".

There was a huge chain reaction. One recipient sent the names of others who would like to receive a letter. Chaplains would pass on lists of names. Agnes soon had to develop a card index system to keep track of the thousands of men with whom she corresponded personally. The personal letters were supplemented by a general letter. And so started what became known as the 'blue backs' because of their blue covers – 50 years of monthly letters. Then a special letter for young trainees was requested. These too continued year after year, not a month missed. Even when Agnes was hospitalised with a broken leg, she contrived a way to write. Though tightly strapped to a wooden bed, she could move her arms. So she balanced a notepad above her head and wrote "after the fashion of a fly walking on the ceiling".

When HMS Alert and HMS Discovery were due to go on a three year Arctic Expedition, there was consternation amongst the sailors – how would they get their letters? So Agnes sat down and wrote 36 letters, one for each month they would be away and then arranged for them to be loaded on board, sealed in tin-lined tea chests, bound in monthly batches. So prolific was her output that there was a stack of prepared letters which were sent out for almost two years after her death. The sheer scale of this work was incredible and it grew each year. By 1905/6, some 745,980 monthly letters were being dispatched.

The effort and thought behind such kindness was much appreciated by the sailors on board. Not surprisingly, they were keen to meet their correspondent in person on their return to English shores. It was some of the early recipients who beseeched Agnes to meet them on their return to Devonport. After some hesitation, she agreed to go.

This visit to Devonport in 1873 shaped Agnes's future in many ways. Not only did she meet her sailor correspondents, she also met a young lady, Sophia Wintz, who was to become her steadfast partner. The two had actually been at the same event a year earlier but had not been introduced. Nevertheless, Agnes had been struck by Sophia's appearance. "Young, fair, golden-haired, the embodiment of health and vigour," was how she described Sophia in her autobiography.

The invitation from an unknown lady to address a meeting of sailors' wives whilst in Devonport, and an offer of accommodation from the lady's mother, brought the two women together – for the unknown lady was indeed Sophia. "We became friends at once, and have continued friends ever since," declared Agnes. The closeness of the pair was accepted by all, including royalty, seemingly without much comment. The Duke of Edinburgh, when Commander-in-Chief at Devonport, did remark that it was splendid to find two women "rowing in one boat all these years, and never capsizing her". In *My Life among the Blue-Jackets,* Agnes even went so far as to refer to "our silver wedding happiness" in 1898, as the couple marked 25 years from their first meeting and the start of their work together.

Whilst Agnes didn't come from a naval family, Sophia's family had connections with the services and her brother Lewis rose to the rank of Admiral. Sophia had been born in Switzerland but the family eventually settled in the Stoke area of Devonport (one of the three towns which now make up the City of Plymouth). She did the Seasons in Bath and attracted the attentions of a young army officer. However, Sophia clearly had doubts and called off their engagement, deciding instead to devote herself to the service of those less fortunate than herself. She had a flair for organizing which complemented Agnes's skills and the two shared a deep religious faith and warm compassion for others.

Yet their first joint venture, to provide some recreational facility for the young sailor boys from the training ships, was almost a disaster. They had seen the need – for the young lads were allowed ashore on Sunday afternoons but left to wander aimlessly around, which meant they often got themselves in to trouble. Their commanding officers tried to deter the two well-meaning ladies from arranging anything, saying the lads preferred their liberty to being organized. Undeterred, Agnes and Sophia hired the Mechanics Hall in Devonport for a meeting, offering free buns. Just one young lad turned up that first week and he fled rapidly. A month on, there was still no interest. It was Sophia's mother who rescued the situation, suggesting that the young sailor boys might prefer a more homely setting. She offered use of her own kitchen. Word soon spread of a warm welcome there and the ladies' work had begun.

It was also about this time that Agnes had an embarrassing experience which caused her to examine her conscience and to start practising what she was preaching. She was fast gaining a reputation as an excellent speaker. Her friend, Miss Williams, ran a mission in Bath and asked Agnes to give a talk about the importance of temperance. It was an unruly group and Agnes found it difficult to hold their attention but she persevered and was duly rewarded when, at the end, several came forward to sign the pledge. However, one man, somewhat the worse for wear, but encouraged by his friends to sign, suddenly challenged Agnes as to whether she herself had taken the pledge. Agnes could do nothing but answer honestly – "No". The man, unsurprisingly, retorted, "Then if you haven't signed, neither will I."

Years later Agnes discovered that not only had this incident made her sign the pledge, it had also sparked something in her challenger. One of Agnes's colleagues was giving a talk and recounting this tale. A chimney sweep, Frank Stephens, was in the audience and identified himself as the man in the story. Although he'd been obstructive on the night, Agnes's words had got through to him and made him think. He'd subsequently become an abstainer.

Agnes offered to help the National Temperance League (NTL) with their work, especially within the Navy. It was Mr Sims, an

NTL organizer, who first suggested that Agnes might talk to sailors on board their ships. This was totally unprecedented and high level permission was required. The Admiral was cautious, despite Agnes's promise that she would address the sailors "as a mother". He compromised, allowing her to hold a lunchtime meeting in the Devonport dockyard. If this went well, if the men were interested and she didn't lose her dignity or say anything which offended, then she would be allowed on board ships. The chaplain would attend and report back. Thankfully for all concerned, the dockyard meeting went well, the chaplain was impressed and the Admiral gave his consent.

That first occasion, on board HMS Impregnable, must have been very daunting for the 32 year old Agnes. All the young sailor boys were sitting on the quarter deck. Agnes stood with the Captain and officers on the poop deck. She later recalled how the only sound, apart from her own voice "was the screech of gulls as they circled and swooped around the ship". But her words found their mark. Over 250 lads signed the pledge and whilst no-one, especially Agnes, was naive enough to think that all would keep it, it was a huge achievement.

It was also the beginning of an impressive programme of visits to ships and other naval establishments, including coastguard stations. When HMS Crocodile returned to Plymouth, Agnes was delighted to meet her very first naval correspondent, George Brown, the sick-berth attendant who had been so jealous of a soldier's letter.

Thankfully, Agnes was a good sailor, often visiting ships in bad weather. "If it was possible to send for me I felt in honour bound to go," she wrote.

One of Agnes's favourite stories was how, on board HMS Topaze she had needed a table on which to place the pledge book. Although the Captain offered to have one sent from his cabin, Agnes didn't want to lose the moment and so commandeered what she thought was the bread tub to act as a make-shift table. To the great amusement of the sailors, it was the grog tub she had spied. The irony of using it to assist sailors to renounce alcohol was appreciated by everyone.

Branches of the NTL were already established on some ships. Then, in 1873, the Royal Naval Temperance Society (RNTS) was formed with support from the NTL and Agnes was appointed its superintendent.

The RNTS's pledge card showed a picture of St George slaying the dragon. The sailor would "pledge my word & honour, God helping me, to abstain from all intoxicating drinks and from taking up rum as a ration". The tradition of the daily rum allowance dated back to 1687, although by the mid 1800s, the rum was watered down and had become known as 'grog'. A meagre cash alternative of a penny farthing was available. Agnes campaigned for an increase in this sum, suggesting tuppence a day in lieu of the rum but it wasn't until after her death that an allowance of three pence a day was made – an offer taken up by many. In 1881, the grog ration was discontinued for officers – a belated recognition by the Admiralty of the dangers of alcohol. Amazingly, it was not until 1970 that the whole system was abolished.

The registrar, or keeper of the pledge-book on board, had to send quarterly returns to the NTL office, giving the numbers of new recruits and backsliders. Stars of merit were awarded to the commander of any ship where ten per cent or more of the crew were members of the temperance society. Medals were awarded to those who had successfully kept their pledge for five years, with bars added for each further five years' abstinence.

Agnes continued to write her monthly letters to thousands of sailors but she also started a monthly journal *Ashore & Afloat* which became extremely popular with a circulation of a quarter of a million at its height. Sophia took on the editor's role. Each month there were stories, often featuring the brave exploits of sailors past and present. There were reports of meetings, letters received from sailors, pithy words of wisdom, for example: "If you want to have a year of comparative happiness, eat less, drink less, smoke less, and think less about getting rich".

There were jokes a-plenty:

'What made you steal the waterproof cloak' demanded the judge. The culprit whispered, 'I was trying to lay up something for a rainy day.'

Why are ladies like churches? There is no living without them; there is many a spire (aspire) to them; and they have a loud clapper in their upper storey.

There were even recipes. As the years went by, there were also regular appeals for funds, especially after some naval disaster, and even an 'Agony Aunt' column written by Agnes herself under the pseudonym 'Aunt Susan'.

Before long, *Ashore & Afloat* was also being sent to all US naval ships. With her usual strict adherence to protocol, Agnes had sought, and obtained, the full consent and co-operation of the Naval Board in Washington to make this happen. Later, special editions were even started for the Australian and the newly formed Canadian Navy.

Ashore & Afloat wasn't the only thing sent out to sailors abroad. During the Boer War, over £4,000 worth of goods – food parcels, pipes and tobacco, warm socks etc – were dispatched. Imagine what it must have been like to be out fighting in South Africa and to receive a Christmas pudding, in an airtight tin, "With Miss Weston's Best Wishes".

Agnes's workload was already heavy when, in 1874, a deputation from HMS Dryad approached her with the request that she set up a teetotal rest house near the dockyard for sailors. Initially she was reluctant. She knew it would be a lifelong commitment and "quite out of the then received code as to women's work" – an important consideration for a respectable woman from the upper middle classes. The idea of rest houses for sailors was not new, but the concept of a sailors' rest which ran on teetotal lines was unusual.

After praying about the matter and with Sophia's offer of help, Agnes overcame her doubts. They started searching for suitable premises and found a dilapidated shop, near the dockyard gates at Devonport. It was surrounded by pubs. Using her own money, Agnes rented the shop for a year, with an option to buy at the end of the lease.

The two women had a clear idea of what they wanted to create – a warm, bright, comfortable and clean space, with good food. But that would cost money. So Agnes wrote letters appealing for funds to various temperance magazines. The *Christian* magazine was particularly supportive and promoted the cause. Soon money started to flow in. One anonymous donor offered to add £5 for every £100 collected. Whilst Sophia got on with all the practical arrangements, Agnes embarked on a speaking tour of Britain to raise more funds, collecting over £1,000 in Scotland alone.

Sophia initially also took responsibility for the accounts but soon a young accountant, Arthur Uren, offered his assistance. He probably didn't realize he would still be doing the task 40 years on, even though the amounts and complexity of the various funds increased significantly. Inevitably, Agnes and Sophia would face accusations, usually from the liquor trade, that they lined their own pockets but they were meticulous in their record-keeping. 'Subscription Lists and Balance Sheets', effectively annual reports, were audited and published each year. Everything was open to scrutiny. Agnes and Sophia always paid for their own keep and travel costs. At first they took all major decisions themselves but, perhaps wisely, they later established a board of trustees to oversee the growing operations. Both women were 'do-ers' and not keen on committees. As they were fond of quoting, "If Noah had had a committee, he would never have built the ark."

Soon the Devonport Rest was ready for business. Agnes resisted the temptation for a grand launch. There was just a simple service of thanksgiving in the adjacent meeting hall on the Sunday prior to the doors opening for custom on 8th May 1876. But three young sailors did persuade her to let them stay that first Sunday evening, so they could have the privilege of being "the first birds to roost there". They later proudly sent Agnes a photograph of themselves taken that evening.

The restaurant was cosy, with bright colours, mirrors and "a little gilding". It clearly aimed to replicate the public house in many ways, just without alcohol. Indeed the reporter from the local paper, *The Western Daily Mercury*, having had a sneak preview two months earlier, wrote that the Rest would "bear minute comparison with the most successful gin palace". A glass panel advertised 'Comfort, Coffee and Company, for One Penny'. The nickname 'The 3 Cs' was soon adopted by the grateful sailors.

The restaurant was open to the general public, providing much needed revenue. Agnes and Sophia aimed to make the place self-supporting. Members of the School of Cookery at South Kensington came to train the cooks. However the recreation areas – smoking room, reading and writing rooms – were restricted to sailors, merchant seamen and soldiers. They just paid for their food, bed and bath (if taken!) There were only 70 sleeping rooms ('cabins' as they were inevitably called) at this point and demand for them was high. In the first year alone, 127,000 servicemen had visited The Rest and over 10,000 men had spent a night there. Once the initial debt was paid off, the priority was for more beds. A tall block of dormitories was later built in the garden.

To add to the homely feel, there was a parrot, Polly, and a retriever, Hector. Polly would greet guests with "Walk in, Jack; glad to see you; have a cup of coffee." But sadly the bird was too popular, killed by the kindness of sailors feeding her all the wrong things.

The dog became a well-known sight in the area, even learning to swim out to ships to greet the men.

Agnes and Sophia had been determined to live on site, to the horror of many of their friends, who declared the pair "should be dead in a year if we were mad enough to live there". They fitted up two small tenement rooms at their own expense. But their friends had been right and it was not long before first Sophia's health, then Agnes's, suffered. They were forced to move out for a while and take a recuperative break in Wales but as the renovation works progressed they were able to move to better rooms within the building.

Of course not all the sailors who came to the Rest were sober. Some were brought along by their mates, very much the worse for wear. But Agnes would always welcome them in. For everyone was "some mother's son" and everyone needed shelter, warmth and sustenance. Inevitably some criticized Agnes for this attitude but she always maintained her stance. Indeed, it wasn't unknown for Agnes herself to bring in some drunken sailor she had found wandering the streets. It was often said that when the pub turned the sailors out, the Rest took them in. The only 'rules' in the Rest were 'no disorderly conduct' and that the guests had to go quietly to bed – so one can imagine the furtive manhandling of inebriated mates along the corridors to a vacant cabin, staff going along with the notion that a strong coffee had sobered 'Jack' sufficiently for him to crash out peacefully.

Neither did the customers have to be Christians. If they chose to attend Bible meetings and services, that was excellent. But it wasn't compulsory. Some men clearly thought attending a short religious talk was a small price to pay for excellent food and lodging. The women believed they constantly saw God's hand at work and that many men found faith as a result of their visits to the Rest or by reading *Ashore & Afloat*. The Royal Navy Christian Union, for

Christians of all denominations, soon established its headquarters at the Rest and even formed its own band there.

In 1878, Agnes and Sophia opened a smaller Rest, 'The Homeward Bound' at Keyham, near Devonport, at the gates of the steam-yard, as it was then known (Around a quarter of naval vessels at that time were steam-driven and needed special facilities to have their engines overhauled.) Described initially as a "branch establishment" of the Devonport Rest, the Keyham site too would later be remodelled and extended.

The success of the Devonport Rest led to requests to open a similar venture for sailors at Portsmouth, where Sarah Robinson (see previous chapter) was working so effectively on behalf of soldiers. The two women were quite different in temperament. Sarah would act and then worry about the funding. Agnes was much more cautious and would not countenance any extension of her work to Portsmouth until the debt on Devonport was cleared. So Sarah had set up a small Sailors' rest in the town but was very keen for Agnes to take over the enterprise. It was the loss of HMS Eurydice, a training frigate, sunk in a squall just off the Isle of Wight which finally persuaded Agnes she must do something in Portsmouth, as the town was so badly affected by the tragedy. Sarah provided her with accommodation and encouragement while she made her plans.

An old music hall with two small houses and a tiny shop, complete with rats, was secured in Commercial Road, Portsmouth – very much as a trial. Sophia and Agnes both moved temporarily to Portsmouth and lived in cramped rooms on site. A coffee shop and reading room were provided but no beds. In the old music hall, Saturday night entertainments were held – bands, recitations, strong men all on the bill. Despite criticism from some quarters, Agnes was convinced that good entertainment was necessary to draw sailors in. She tried to ensure it remained 'wholesome', presiding over each session herself. In her autobiography, she admitted she was sometimes hoodwinked by the innocent-sounding title of a song but she became adept at calling a halt to proceedings when she detected anything of a dubious nature.

Inevitably, the need for larger premises grew. A local carpenter told Sophia about a potential site just along Commercial Road and Agnes was immediately attracted to it. Uncharacteristically she made an offer, without having the wherewithal to pay. But providentially the following day she was asked to speak at a drawing-room meeting in London by one of her supporters, Anthony Denny. At the outset, he asked Agnes what she needed. She answered honestly, but with no great expectations, "£1,000". By the end of the evening she had raised 1,000 guineas. Her prayers had been answered.

In June 1881, the Portsmouth Sailors' Rest was formally opened – not by some dignitary but by the sailors themselves. From the start, it was the sailors who pledged to keep their Rest going, helping with fund-raising and classes. There was no money for a big hall, so a large marquee was erected in the courtyard. But, just as in Devonport, the buildings and facilities grew over the years. Ultimately there would be a fine Diamond Jubilee Block and a Beresford Block, providing some 600 beds. It must have been very satisfying to erect such facilities on the site of a notorious pub, the French Maid, acquired when its licence was not renewed. Business was brisk. A typical weekend would see 2,000 eggs and 3,000 bread rolls devoured.

Amongst the facilities provided were safe storage lockers, bath cubicles where towels were warmed on radiators (the height of luxury) and a barbers. Sailors back from long voyages could stay and become 'human' again before returning to their families.

It can't have been easy, running large establishments as far afield as Plymouth and Portsmouth. Agnes and Sophia gradually gathered together a good team of volunteer helpers, including many women such as Miss Brown, later a trustee, who stayed loyal to their cause for decades. Paid employment was often given to ex-servicemen or to sailor's wives. The business of the meeting halls was run independently from the hospitality side. There would be two shifts of workers, for day and night, with no-one working longer than 10 hours at a time. On Sundays, all staff would get at least a half-day off. By 1905, there were some 170 workers, across the three Rests. At 5.30, 6.00 and 6.30 every morning, the night-watchman would ring a bell, rousing the sailors in time for their return to their ships. They'd swapped 'last orders' for 'last call'.

Whilst the local police were usually supportive, the local brewers, and the local prostitutes, were not. One opponent described Agnes's work as "a disgraceful innovation which ought to be crushed by all right-thinking men". Agnes refused to get too concerned about the hostility. She merely increased the insurance for the premises in case of trouble.

Agnes quickly adopted the Navy's attitude that there was no such word as 'impossible'. When she needed to expand at Devonport, the presence of three pubs between the Rest and the Dockyard gates might have been seen as a hindrance. But not to Agnes. She managed to acquire all three pubs, helped by two generous donations of £1,000 each. One of these came from Robert Whitehead, the inventor of the Whitehead torpedo, sent so she could "knock a hole in one of the pubs!" He probably also appreciated Agnes's claim that "you don't make a torpedo gunner out of a drunkard". Amongst many smaller donations was a sovereign wrapped in silver paper – Agnes was touched to find it was from a young bride-to-be; the enclosed note explaining that it was only because of the Rest and Agnes's help that her fiancé had saved enough for their first home.

The new Devonport building, which opened in 1888, had a grand frontage, with a turret and a weather vane in the shape of an old Viking ship. To support the planning application, Agnes had written to the Chairman of the Board of works saying, "I am desirous that the new buildings should be an ornament and a credit to the town, and shall spare no pain or money to make them so." Large dormitories were divided by varnished wooden partitions into eight foot by five foot cabins, most having their own window. By 1890, the building occupied a massive 6,300 square feet.

There was a separate wing for the naval trainees. Often over 200 would gather there for tea. Sunday services were always over within the hour. Agnes didn't wish to challenge anyone's attention span. She reinforced her messages with pithy mottos on the walls: "Imitate the best, not the worst" and "The more you think, the less you'll drink".

The other major naval dockyard in the south was Chatham and Agnes could often be found holding meetings there. She also worked closely with the Royal Hospital School in Greenwich, a centre for navigation and seamanship instruction. A sailor boy at the school commented about the monthly letters he received, "I think that if everybody was to do what every letter told them to do, they would not go far wrong." Agnes was clearly providing a moral compass for the trainees.

In 1892, Agnes and Sophia organized a stand at the Royal Naval exhibition in the grounds of Chelsea Hospital. They made a mock-up of a full-sized cabin, complete with furniture. Outside it, by the flag pole, stood the lifelike figure of a sailor looking through a telescope. The exhibition ran for 151 days so a temporary Sailors' Rest was set up to provide restaurant facilities and a reading and writing room. The attendant publicity brought in more funds, all used to support widows and orphans of sailors.

Agnes promoted temperance by appealing to sailors and supporters' sense of duty to family, to God and to the country. She didn't mince her words about the culture of drinking within the

Navy. "Drink has always been the seamen's snare ... the cause of nearly all the crime in the service," she wrote in an article about her work. "To see the fine, manly, stalwart form of a man-o'-war's man reeling up the street, all his manliness gone, and the kindly, pleasant-spoken fellow turned either into a drivelling idiot or a rough swearing bully, is a spectacle sad enough to make men and angels weep."

Some of Agnes's rhetoric about sailors was not always well-received by the sailors themselves. By the early 1900s, there had been major improvements in general behaviour in the navy. The editor of *The Bluejacket* newspaper, Lionel Yexley, didn't think Agnes's words reflected this. He led the protests over her portrayal of a sailor as someone who could ignore his duty to his family in pursuit of drunken pleasure. It seemed Yexley and his supporters had grown tired of Agnes's hectoring tone. They didn't want to be 'mothered' but "to be treated more like men". But this criticism was not widespread.

In 1901, Agnes was granted an honorary degree from the University of Glasgow, one of the first four women to be given such an award. The Scots had always been very supportive of her work and Agnes was extremely proud of this honour.

By 1905, with the opening of the new Victoria Memorial Building at Devonport, over £250,000 had been raised and spent on buildings at Portsmouth, Devonport and Keyham. That's over £25 million in today's terms. Figures given in the 1905/6 Subscription List and Balance Sheet show that, in that year alone, 159,637 beds had been let in Portsmouth, 148,582 in Devonport and 22,804 in Keyham. Total meals taken were 225,840 in Portsmouth, 326,906 in Devonport and 80,521in Keyham. These were clearly very sizeable enterprises and they continued to expand. There had also been two smaller rests at Portland and Sheerness, but when the leases ran out on these buildings, Agnes chose not to renew them. Perhaps she was conscious of the dangers of spreading her efforts too thinly, geographically at least.

As Admiral Lord Charles Beresford said, "… all that money has been got together by the energy and unselfish work – voluntary work – of Miss Weston and Miss Wintz." No wonder he declared that the Rests "are of great good to the state". Indeed, WS Caine, MP and Civil Lord of the Admiralty, estimated that Agnes's work saved the country £1 million per year.

Impressive and important as the physical buildings were, it was the services provided within and reaching out from the Rests which had the biggest impact on the ordinary lives of the blue-jackets and their families. Working so closely with sailors, Agnes became acutely aware of their problems and saw they were not all caused by drink. Some arose, she felt, as a direct consequence of the Admiralty's own rules and regulations.

When a sailor went abroad, he not only had to buy all his own kit and uniform; his pay was changed from weekly to monthly and two months' money was 'retained' in case he deserted. So it was three months later before his wife or mother could draw their half-pay, the other half being set aside for the men themselves. Meanwhile, the families would have nothing to live on. Starvation and eviction always threatened. Agnes campaigned tirelessly for changes. Eventually the Admiralty allowed wages to be drawn at the end of the first month, but this still left several weeks with no money coming in.

To make matters worse, the half-pay had to be collected by the wives in person at the dockyard. Yet not everyone lived locally. It was often wet and cold and the queues were long. Agnes thought this outrageous. Her campaigning led to the matter being raised in Parliament and a Royal Commission was set up to look into the matter. Agnes and Sophia gave evidence. They also supported many sailor's wives and mothers to give their own personal testimonies.

Good sense prevailed and by 1895 the system was changed. The half-pay would in future be sent by monthly draft, cashable at the family's local Post Office.

Sailors' wages were not exactly generous. Agnes took a three pronged approach to this problem. She set up classes at the Rests so the men could study and get better qualified, so able to try for promotion or at least get badges to increase their pay. She hired instructors to teach specialist subjects. In effect, she was doing a lot of the Navy's work for them.

She encouraged the men to take their savings home, not spend them as soon as they returned from their postings. She tried, but failed, to get the authorities to set up a dockyard savings bank. Although eventually a Dockyard Post Office was opened at Devonport, Agnes decided to take matters into her own hands. She set up savings accounts at the Devonport Rest. She calculated that over £84,000 passed through her hands as she acted on behalf of single men, drawing their half pay. She would send out whatever they requested and save the remainder until their return. Needless to say, every penny was strictly accounted for. She also organized for sailors to buy their railway tickets for home whilst still aboard their ship, so the money didn't get squandered in the port.

Agnes's third strategy was to help sailors' wives, or better still, to help them help themselves. Each Monday afternoon, the Rests in Devonport and Portsmouth would be filled with hundreds of women. Crèche and nursery facilities were provided, while talks, concerts and short Bible readings were held. The wives were assisted to run their own coal, thrift, boot and sick clubs. Each year a two day bazaar would be held, each stall named after a ship and a model HMS Agnes Weston manned by children. The bazaar would close with a giant jumble sale and often raised more than £200.

Some of the money raised provided a holiday home in the Saltash area, where needy families could go for a two week break.

Other funds would go to the Victoria Jubilee Nurses Association, so enabling sailors' wives to get immediate medical attention when required. Pregnant wives were encouraged to save at least £1 towards their confinement expenses, although Agnes also ensured the Rest added a little bit extra so the families had sufficient food during this time. In the summer, outings for sailors' wives would be organized, with the children being looked after at the Rests. What joy this must have brought to the women who battled on so bravely whilst their husbands were away.

Eventually branches of the Royal Naval Temperance Society and the Royal Navy Christian Union were formed for women. Initially women had not been eligible for these societies so Agnes had started a branch of the British Women's Temperance Association (BWTA) in Devonport. Agnes was very impressed by the work being done by Lady Henry Somerset, as President of the BWTA. She would often address BWTA meetings and also supported the World Woman's Christian Temperance Union (WWCTU). At the Union's international conference in London in June 1895, Agnes was on the platform. She presented medals to a group of sailors to mark their continued abstinence and declared that one in six men in the Navy were now teetotallers – a very high percentage given the prevailing culture. When Lady Henry was setting up her village at Duxhurst in 1894 for the recovery of inebriate women (see Chapter 9), Agnes was keen to assist. She organized her BWTA branch members, plus sailors and officers, to raise funds for a cottage at Duxhurst, demonstrating their willingness to help others.

Agnes called upon her supporters to join the Royal Sailors' Rest Needlework Guild and to contribute at least two garments a year which were then sold, very cheaply, at the women's meetings. Some fine garments flowed in, for patrons included royalty, aristocracy and admirals' wives. Toys were recycled in a similar way. By 1906, the Guild had some 2,250 members. Sailors' wives also made garments in special workrooms at the Rests. These were then sold to generate funds. The Prince of Wales once ordered 30 garments from the workrooms to be distributed to poor parishes, thus doubling the philanthropic effect.

The behaviour of young sons often proved a challenge to wives whilst their husbands were at sea. So Agnes established a Boys Naval Brigade, persuading several qualified instructors to help out teaching the lads sports, drills, signalling and compass work. It was run with Navy discipline – attendance at all parades and drills was compulsory and poor behaviour could result in dismissal. Although the caps had to be purchased, the uniform was provided by Agnes and was expected to last three years. Certificates were awarded for regular attendance and training. These could later provide exemption from some months of training if the boys then joined the navy itself – 'a win/win situation', as it would be called today.

A young lad called Charles Jemmett belonged to the Brigade in 1910, before he was suddenly struck down by a brain haemorrhage, aged just 11. Agnes immediately wrote to his parents, taking time to praise the boy for his excellent character and attention to duty. She offered "any mark of respect and affection that the Corps can pay" – an offer which resulted in the boy's coffin being borne on a gun carriage and escorted to the church by the Brigade cadets. It was a gesture typical of Agnes and summarised the whole philosophy of the Royal Sailors' Rests – everyone, whatever their age, was 'family' and deserved respect in death, as in life.

Daughters weren't forgotten either. A girls' branch of the RNTS soon followed, providing excursions, Bible classes and First Aid instruction.

Then there was the Employment Bureau, possibly one of the first of its kind. The aim was to find work for men leaving the navy. But it also helped sailors' widows, for the wife's half-pay stopped immediately on a sailor's death. Agnes campaigned tirelessly for sailors' widows' pensions but she was impatient with bureaucracy and also took immediate action to help stricken families when disaster struck.

Her early experience of hospital visiting in Bath came in useful as Agnes spent a lot of time visiting bereaved naval families. When, in November 1890, HMS Serpent sank two days out of Plymouth, with only three of the 176 crew surviving, Devonport was devastated by grief. Many wives and mothers descended on the office of the Commander-in-Chief, at that time the Duke of Edinburgh. He immediately called in both Agnes and Sophia, along with Major Quill of the Soldiers' and Sailors' Families Association. Together they formed a committee to collect money for the bereaved families. Over £13,000 was raised, and used, very quickly. Pensions were provided for wives and mothers with a sum of money invested for each child. Not all bereaved families were local, so great efforts were made, including through newspaper advertisements, to trace all those affected. In a letter to *The Times*, Agnes wrote, "The Admiralty have kindly given me every information, my workers have visited all local cases, and the distant ones are being looked into by the clergy, who are kindly reporting their circumstances to me ... I am anxious to do the work thoroughly and well ..."

So well did she do the work that this process became a model for future naval disasters, of which, sadly, there were many. The greatest peacetime tragedy was the loss of HMS Victoria in 1893 when 371 men died. The Portsmouth Rest became a crisis centre, opening its doors to all the bereaved. Very practical, immediate help was offered; rent paid when bailiffs came knocking, mourning clothes provided, pensions set up. The Royal Patriotic Commission had been established to deal with such matters but it was thirteen months after the disaster before their first pensions were paid out. Meanwhile, Agnes had breached the gap, raising almost £70,000 to provide much needed relief. As Father Dolling, a great supporter of

Agnes, wrote in *Ten years in the Slums*, "the charity of the nation is strangled by the red tape of officialdom ... I believe that if it had not been for Miss Weston many would have actually died from starvation."

It wasn't just the Patriotic Fund's "reprehensible tardiness" which attracted Agnes's ire. In a letter to *The Times,* she complained about the cost of its administration, in the order of 13/8d per head, compared to the 6d per head of her own Serpent Fund.

Sailors from foreign fleets were always welcome at the Rests and Agnes and Sophia were always welcome on board their vessels in port. Indeed the Germans, French and Japanese were all so impressed by what they saw that they decided to replicate the idea in their own countries. When the Japanese ship Katori was in Portsmouth in 1906, Agnes was presented with a Japanese translation of one of her own booklets, *Underneath the Searchlight*. It is amazing to think that this account of how she had established the Devonport Rest had been used as a blueprint for six similar facilities on the far side of the world. Agnes was even invited out to Japan to see them for herself, an invitation she declined due to lack of time. But she was clearly thrilled by her efforts at international fellowship and a picture of Japanese sailors at the Rest was used on the front cover of the 1905/6 Subscription List. Similar photographs were included in her autobiography. Rather poignantly, the 1909/10 Subscription List included a photograph of three sailors, with the caption "How the English Sailor made the Japanese and Russian men shake hands at Portsmouth".

In 1909, 500 sailors from the Russian fleet were entertained at a reception at the Portsmouth Rest, hosted by Sophia. The Americans, too, were regular visitors.

Sadly, World War One would change the atmosphere. It pained Agnes greatly that her German friends and supporters were suddenly 'the enemy'. But the Rests provided welcome facilities for all allied fleets and housed women workers and nurses from the colonies and the USA. After the battle of Jutland in 1916, Agnes sent out over 5,000 letters of sympathy. She not only felt the public grief; there was personal loss, with the death of her own nephew, John Weston, to whom she had been very close.

During the war, the Rests became an invaluable resource, thrown open to soldiers as well as sailors. The halls were turned into club rooms, providing writing materials, games, books and a quiet sanctuary. There were often entertainments, with music and films. And always there would be coffee and cake and a friendly word. Agnes tried to ensure every man going off to war received a little gift such as a writing compendium or a warm muffler. Over 5,000 Bibles and Gospels were given out. She described the first year of the war as like "a bad dream" but she never let up in her efforts. "We sometimes feel ourselves tired *in* the work, but never tired *of* the work," she wrote.

Months before similar restrictions were imposed throughout the country, the Plymouth Fortress Commander applied controls on the sale of alcohol in the town. In August 1914, all pubs in the area were closed for six weeks. Later, opening hours were restricted and servicemen were not allowed in until noon. The Rests, however, were always open and always provided a friendly welcome.

The Plymouth and West Devon History Centre holds an account written by B Hart recalling the Devonport Rest shortly after war broke out. " … if you didn't book a bed as soon as you went ashore it was difficult to get one, especially when all the ships were in port." If all the beds were full, the sailors would sleep on seats and on the floors but "no charge was made for this". The lockers were often used to keep a 'civvy suit' in, for sailors were required to wear their uniforms to go ashore. "I have spent some happy times at Aggys (sic) as it was generally known to all sailors," reminisced Mr Hart. He also remembered how Miss Weston "would do anything to help them [sailors] when in trouble even to going on board ship to see their captain to try and settle their trouble ..." This sailor was clearly an admirer of Agnes's work. So it is perhaps fitting that, having just returned to the naval barracks from a long duty on board a destroyer, he was one of the men detailed to line the grave at Agnes's funeral, to fire off three volleys into the air, before the last post was sounded.

Agnes was much impressed by the work women did during the war. She argued that women should have the right to vote but she was no suffragette. Violent protest was not her style. She also firmly believed that women should be at home when their young children returned from school. However, Plymouth struck its own blow for sexual equality when in 1919, Nancy Astor was elected as MP for the town and became the first woman to take her seat in the House of Commons.

Agnes's work most certainly benefitted from the support of the Royal family. This was a reflection not only of the value of the work but also of the involvement of many of the royal princes in the navy itself. Prince Edward and Prince George had visited informally when serving as naval cadets. The first official royal visit had been by the Princess Royal in 1887, to mark the Queen's Golden Jubilee. This led to a gift of 30 guineas to endow a cabin in the name of her son, Prince Henry of Prussia, himself a sailor. When serving as Commander-in-Chief at Plymouth, the Duke of Edinburgh developed a close working relationship with Agnes and Sophia, especially following naval disasters. He recognized that, over the previous two decades, there had been a big improvement in the conduct of sailors, with a notable reduction in offences of insubordination. This, he believed, was due not only to better training, but to greater sobriety and for that Agnes deserved much credit.

Queen Victoria herself was so impressed by what she was hearing that she summoned Agnes to an audience at Windsor. Another meeting at Osborne House followed. In 1892, the Queen granted the Rests her Royal Warrant and they became known as the 'Royal Sailors' Rests' – a massive tribute to the work of two remarkable women – Agnes and Sophia. Agnes's cycling accident in 1896, which resulted in a two month hospital stay, even got a mention in the Court Circular. Once the Duchess of Edinburgh paid an informal visit to the Devonport Rest, going around incognito talking to the sailor boys and serving coffee. However word soon got out (the Royal Ensign flying above the building proved a bit of a giveaway!) and many more crowded in to see the royal visitor.

This royal support continued after Queen Victoria's death. In June 1910, the King and Queen became official patrons of the Sailors' Rests. On Trafalgar Day in 1913, Agnes was presented by the Duchess of Albany with an illuminated address. As Agnes proudly recounted in her book, it was signed by "most of the well-known names in England, together with representatives of the great lines of steamships, and leading and distinguished naval officers".

It is probably this royal endorsement over many decades which ensured that Agnes, 'The Sailors' Friend' has been remembered more than Sarah Robinson, 'The Soldiers' Friend'. For Agnes had friends in high places and worked hard to cultivate their on-going interest. Sarah, perhaps because of her disabilities but also due to her own temperament, was less inclined to fraternize with high society.

After Agnes's death in 1918, her partner Sophia continued with the work. She raised funds for a new accommodation block at Devonport as a memorial to Agnes. She reiterated their mantra, "A Sober Navy is a National Insurance". Finances became tight in the post war years and the price of cabins had to be doubled, to 1/- a night. *Ashore & Afloat* was still going strong, with a circulation of over 600,000.

Sophia's contribution to the tremendous work of the Sailors' Rests and associated activities was recognized when she, too, became a Dame in 1920. She was also granted the honour of a naval funeral on her death in January 1921 and laid to rest beside her friend Agnes. Sophia's obituary in *The Times* talked of her "great intellectual vigour and capacity ... an unaffected, charming personality, which endeared her to all associated with her." One of Agnes's nephews, Charles Weston, had already become involved as trustee and it was he who continued to manage the Rests after Sophia's death.

The Devonport Rest was blitzed during the Second World War. A new Rest was built in the 1960s and there are many families in Plymouth who have fond memories of it – some ex-sailors can even still quote their locker numbers. However the need for overnight accommodation for sailors ashore declined and the Rest closed.

But outreach work for the welfare of the sailor continues to this day. Even in 2014, the objectives of the Dame Agnes Weston's Royal Sailors Rests, or 'Aggie's', as it is more affectionately known, still include "the cause of temperance by providing accommodation and facilities for recreation and other Christian outreach work, without alcohol being provided or consumed". That's quite a legacy!

CHAPTER 8

Catherine Booth (1829 – 1890) 'Mother of The Salvation Army'

It would be impossible to write about Catherine Booth without reference to her husband, William. Yet, amazingly, some historians have tried to write about William and the Salvation Army without any real consideration of Catherine – or her views on drink, duty and women in the church. This chapter aims to redress that balance, without purporting in any way to be a detailed history of the couple's great creation, the Salvation Army.

To Salvationists, Catherine is endearingly known as the 'mother' of the Salvation Army. She had very strong views on the perils of drink. She didn't understand the meaning of the word 'moderation'. For her, only total abstinence would do. By the age of 16, Catherine had already decided she would only marry a teetotaller – someone who abstained on principle, not out of deference to her.

Folklore and myth abound in the history of The Salvation Army and the story of its founders. Early biographies of Catherine by Frederick Booth-Tucker, their son-in-law, and of William by Harold Begbie were sanitised, almost fawning, tributes to their heroes. More recently, Roy Hattersley has given us *Blood & Fire – William and Catherine Booth and their Salvation Army*, a more rounded interpretation which dares to pose some interesting questions about the 'cult-like' activities of the early Salvationists.

I was therefore intrigued and delighted to discover that the Salvation Army International Heritage Centre held a copy of Catherine's own *Reminiscences*, transcribed and edited in 2005 by

David Bennett. Sadly Catherine died whilst still dictating her memoirs so these are an incomplete account of her work and life. There are many blanks with notations to check dates or specific events but these *Reminiscences* do seem to have been intended for publication. In the event, they formed the basis for Frederick Booth-Tucker's book. In going back to Catherine's own words, I felt that I was stripping away a layer of 'spin' and getting closer to the real woman.

Catherine Mumford, born in Ashbourne, Derbyshire in 1829 was, in many ways, an unusual child. Her mother was devoutly religious and refused for many years to send Catherine to school for fear she would be tainted by association with people of less pure views. Her father also used to preach occasionally and was a member of a temperance society.

In her childhood, and indeed throughout her life, Catherine suffered many illnesses, including back and heart problems, but used her periods of incapacitation to study the Bible and theological texts. Her detailed knowledge of the scriptures, acquired in her youth when she was banned from reading novels, would stand her in good stead in her future work. She could always find some Biblical quote to support her arguments.

By the age of 12, she was already secretary of a juvenile temperance society. She would write impassioned letters to the temperance magazines to which her father subscribed, apparently using a *nom de plume*. This was not mere youthful arrogance. Catherine was already displaying her obdurate nature, her unwillingness to compromise her principles.

By the time she was 16, Catherine, now living in Brixton, London, was taking a class for the Reform Methodists. She experienced her moment of divine intervention when singing a Charles Wesley hymn; she felt an "assurance of salvation" which remained with her for the rest of her life. It was her work with the

Reform Methodists that was to lead to her meeting with William Booth, her future husband.

William, too, was a strong personality, committed even as a teenager to taking God's word to the people, not expecting the people to come to God's traditional churches. Catherine was deeply impressed by the impassioned preaching of the young man when he delivered his first sermon for the Reformers in Binfield Chapel House. She was even more impressed when later, at a gathering over tea at the house of Edward Rabbits (an early patron), William gave a striking rendition of a teetotal poem, *The Grog Seller's Dream*.

This poem had come over with the American evangelists and tells the tale of a publican reflecting on his night's work, serving all the drunkards:

> *"To their drunken slumbers, one by one,*
> *Foolish and fuddled, his friends had gone.*
> *To wake in the morn to a drunkard's pain.*
> *With bloodshot eyes and a reeling brain …*
> *But business is business, and what care I?*
> *Yet I hate to have women coming to me.*
> *With their tweedle-de-dum and their tweedle-de-dee;*
> *With their swollen eyes and their haggard looks,*
> *And their speeches learnt from Temperance Books,*
> *With their pale lean children – the whimpering fools,*
> *Why don't they go to the public schools?*
> *I've a right to engage in a lawful trade,*
> *And to take my chance where there's cash to be made …"*

But falling asleep by the fire, the grogseller then had a vivid dream of a horned devil, who praised the work he was doing.

> *"You rival in mischief the Devil himself!"*

He woke terrified from his dream. Then,

> *"Solemn and thoughtful his bed he sought,*
> *And long on that midnight vision he thought!"*

William had actually been reluctant to recite the poem for fear of offending other guests who weren't teetotal. But his host, Mr Rabbits, who wasn't an abstainer himself, insisted, saying if he wasn't offended then why should others be? Catherine was delighted, though the discussion which followed showed that, at this stage, William wasn't entirely committed to the teetotal cause. He might have taken the pledge as a child but his self-denial had long since lapsed, especially as his mother had encouraged him to take port for the sake of his health. Catherine took him to task, arguing passionately for the need for total abstinence.

Her words might have struck home. For when William had first arrived in London, he had lived with his sister, Ann, and her husband for a short while. But he had been shocked to discover that the couple drank heavily. He found the whole experience of living with them very uncomfortable. So he was driven back to work in pawnbroking, the only employment in which he had previous experience, as this provided lodgings above the shop.

Surprisingly, though William had clearly made an impression on Catherine, she hadn't had the same effect on him. He didn't even seem to remember this first meeting. It was only on a second occasion, again engineered by Rabbits, that William fell "head over heels" in love. On that momentous occasion, William was full of excitement. He had just been offered his first full-time preacher post and here was a woman who could be his perfect companion in his new life – clever, not afraid to share her strong opinions, even if these might be unfashionable, and deeply committed to doing God's work. Catherine must have recognized in William a kindred spirit

– a willingness to defy convention to get things done. Theirs was a true meeting of minds. The couple seemed to realise that together they could be a greater force for good, and for God, than as individuals.

Indeed the couple quickly came to realize their love for each other. Although in no position, financially, to marry, they were engaged just a month after that second meeting. In his book *Blood & Fire – William and Catherine Booth and their Salvation Army*, Roy Hattersley observes that William Booth's "greatest piece of good fortune was meeting and marrying one of the most extraordinary women of the nineteenth century".

Rather touchingly, in a letter Catherine sent to William during their engagement, she wrote, "The thought of walking through life perfectly united, together enjoying its sunshine and battling with its storms, by warmest sympathy sharing every smile and every tear … is to me exquisite happiness; the highest earthly bliss I desire. And who can estimate the glory to God and the benefit to man, accruing from a life spent in such harmonious effort to do His will?"

Although it was several years before they married, as William tried to further his career as an evangelist, the pair wrote to each other constantly. When William admitted to drinking a glass of port "for health reasons", Catherine was scathing in her disapproval, going so far as to send him a book with "several green marks and pencillings" which she urged him to read "even if you sit up an hour later every night till you have done so". She had the tone of a hectoring schoolmarm. "I abominate that hackneyed but monstrously inconsistent tale – a teetotaller in principle, but obliged to take a little for my 'stomach's sake'. Such teetotallers aid the progress of intemperance more than all the drunkards in the land! And there are sadly too many of them among ministers." Perhaps this explains some of her frustrations with the established church.

Yet subsequently she herself confessed, in an almost off-hand manner, to taking "a strong dose of brandy and ginger which made me completely tipsy" when she feared she might have contracted cholera. This time it was William who was shocked. It seems the belief that spirits and fortified wine had medicinal value was hard to shake off even for the very strong-willed.

William and Catherine married in June 1855 but their early life together wasn't easy. However, it would undoubtedly have been harder if they hadn't been so mutually supportive. They had already agreed a set of rules by which they would live, including a promise not to argue in front of their children. They would also "avoid desultory conversation", whilst sharing their religious experiences and providing appropriate advice and support to each other. This might not sound like a recipe for domestic bliss, even in Victorian times, yet for Catherine and William it worked. And one of the reasons for this was that it allowed Catherine a voice, both within the marriage and in the couple's missionary work.

Both Catherine and William were very uncompromising and dogmatic in their views, making them unpopular in some quarters. They switched alliances within various off-shoots of Methodism (Wesleyan, Wesleyan Reform and Congregationalists) to find a better match for their strong evangelical zeal. A more cynical view would be that, at this point of their lives, their aim was to further William's career.

Certainly Congregationalism was a strange choice, for its Calvinistic doctrine of predestination (with the 'elect' preordained for salvation) was far removed from either William or Catherine's views. They believed that God was there for everyone; that anyone could seek, and find, salvation. So, unsurprisingly, the couple didn't remain long within the ranks of the Congregationalists, although it was William who broke away first, withdrawing his application for ordination.

Their next involvement was with the New Connexion, seen as

a more liberal off-shoot of Wesleyan Methodism. But William was developing his own style of evangelism. Catherine saw some dangers in his approach, urging him to be aware of the risk of mass hysteria rather than genuine conversions. If he was in danger of enjoying his success too much, she would always be ready to remind him of the need for humility.

It was perhaps inevitable that, in the future, William would create his own movement, with Catherine not only encouraging him but actively participating. For, as WT Stead, the campaigning journalist and close friend of the couple, wrote in his biographical sketch of Catherine, "The Salvation Army is quite as much the work of Mrs Booth as it is of William."

It was her views on the rights of women to preach which ultimately led to the Salvation Army allowing men and women equal status both as officers and preachers. Initially William had struggled with the notion that women could be religious leaders but he was soon persuaded by Catherine's views, which she naturally backed up with Biblical references. For Catherine was William's intellectual superior and he was usually wise enough to recognise this fact.

Catherine also encouraged William's social conscience and led the drive for practical solutions to the plight of the poor such as the "Food-for-the-Million" shops which provided hot soup and a three course dinner for sixpence.

But it was her conviction that only total abstinence would help people find salvation that steered the Salvation's Army's policy on alcohol. Sadly her own father, once such a staunch advocate of temperance, had succumbed to alcoholism due to emotional and financial pressures. He lost his employment and lost his faith. It is a sad irony that Catherine, whilst personally responsible for encouraging many people to turn to God and away from drink, was unable to save her own father from his downfall.

Despite having her first three children in quick succession, Catherine fully supported her husband's work. Her parenting style could be judged as harsh and socially unacceptable today. She might be revered as the 'mother' of the Salvation Army but what definition of good mothering includes whipping one's child or making their marriage ceremony into a mass rally for which tickets were sold?

In fact Catherine left much of the childcare to her mother. She didn't want the children to have "showy" clothes, lest they became vain even at a young age. Even her mother was shocked when Catherine wrote criticizing clothes she had sent for the baby, because of their frippery. "It would be the most glaring inconsistency if I were to deck out my children as the worldlings do."

Catherine seemed determined to make an example of her 'ordinariness' with her first son, in particular. So though Bramwell's christening was a big affair, this was only because he was one of 30 children being christened that day by William Booth.

The children had to be taught "implicit and uncompromising obedience". This meant that physical punishment was common. Catherine, writing of her first son, Bramwell, admitted, "I believe he will be a thoroughly noble lad if I can preserve him from evil influences ... I have had to whip him thrice lately, severely for disobedience and it has cost me some tears. But it has done some good and I am reaping already the rewards of my self-sacrifice." Sadly, she seems to have been more concerned about the mental anguish the incident caused her than the physical and emotional hurt it caused her young son. On another occasion, she tolerated, even supported, William's suggestion that Bramwell be confined to the attic for a few days if he couldn't behave better and set a good example to his brother and sister.

Despite their heavy workload and often nomadic lifestyle, William and Catherine had eight children in the space of 12 years. But Bramwell, Ballington, Kate, Emma, Herbert, Marion,

Evangeline (Eveline) and Lucy didn't enjoy their parents' time and attention as much as they might have liked. They were rarely permitted to indulge in normal childish pursuits.

Catherine believed all parents had a duty to train their children for "holiness, usefulness and heaven". Roy Hatterseley in his book comments, "Even judged against the behaviour of the most pious Victorian Nonconformists, the Booths' treatment of their children was bizarre." He concludes that it was not surprising the children so frequently suffered illnesses, mental and physical; for "all the children were subject to pressure which their infant minds could not accommodate".

Catherine and William never disguised their lofty ambitions for their offspring – they were all being groomed to become evangelists – to continue the Booth dynasty. The foundations for a great church were being built, but in the developing personalities of the Booth children there was a latent defect already lurking which would create the later rift amongst them.

Whilst still part of the New Connexion movement, the family moved to Gateshead. Catherine became increasingly aware of the social problems around her and was aghast at the way young girls had to work in the mills. She saw nothing ironic in the fact that she treated her own children so harshly. That was for their own good. Girls being sent to work in the mills was unacceptable, as it was for the good of their parents and the mill owners.

She also started working directly with drunkards, doing what she termed "a systematic course of house-to-house visitation" on two evenings a week. It started one Sunday when she came across a woman standing on a door-step, jug in hand. Catherine discovered the woman was caring for a drunken husband. Eventually she talked her way into the house and undeterred by the pitiable state of the man, she began to speak to him "of his present deplorable condition, of the folly and wickedness of his course, of the interests of his wife and children … I read to him the parable of the Prodigal Son, while the tears ran down his face like rain". The following day, she persuaded him to sign the temperance pledge.

Within a few weeks she had persuaded ten drunkards "to abandon their soul-destroying habits, and to meet me once a week for reading Scriptures and for prayer". Already she was recognizing the need for on-going support. She also had a cunning way of finding people to visit. "I used to ask one drunkard's wife where another lived. They always knew," she wrote.

She also became increasingly interested in the work of Dr and Mrs Palmer, travelling American evangelists. Phoebe Palmer proclaimed that a formal rejection of strong drink was an essential element of 'holiness', a sentiment Catherine echoed. Whilst Dr Walter Palmer led services, it was his wife Phoebe who brought them to a dramatic conclusion. When Mrs Palmer was denounced in the local press for having the effrontery, as a mere woman, to preach, Catherine felt compelled to write a pamphlet in support of women preachers, using biblical quotations to support her case. She hadn't, at this stage, preached publically herself, although she was teaching classes of young girls and women. But that moment was soon to come.

In December 1857, Catherine addressed a Band of Hope meeting and recorded afterwards that she "felt quite at home on the platform, far more than I do in the kitchen". She wasn't content just to be a wife and mother when God's work needed to be done.

It was as she recovered from the birth of her fourth child that Catherine felt the divine call to preach. And so it was that at a Whit Sunday service led by her husband, she experienced the urge to go to the front and speak. William, wisely, let her talk and her testimony was well received. In fact, shortly afterwards, in an example of role reversal well ahead of its time, he stayed mainly at home looking after the children whilst Catherine carried out his pastoral duties.

This was publically excused and accepted because of William's apparent illness.

By February 1861, both Catherine and William felt God's calling to work together as peripatetic evangelists. They didn't want to be tied down to one area, or to one master. Their links with the New Connexion were already fraying. In dramatic fashion, they walked out of its annual conference when William didn't get his own way. For the New Connexion wasn't willing to grant him a role solely as an evangelist; they wanted him as a circuit minister with limited permission to preach elsewhere. "Never" was Catherine's apparent response to this attempt to fetter her husband's work. However, a compromise was brokered and for a short while the inevitable split was delayed as William took up a post in Newcastle. Within months, with Catherine's full support, he had resigned. The family might be poor, with no home and little money, but they had huge faith in their destiny – to convert sinners.

The couple went off to Cornwall, leaving the children with Catherine's mother. Even Catherine found the separation hard but her children took second place to what she perceived as her duty to support her husband. One might argue that they actually took third place behind Catherine's own desire to evangelize. For, by her own admission, Catherine was "in my element in the work, and only regret that I did not commence it years ago".

Catherine's preaching was especially well received in the West Country. She also continued her work with drunkards. The couple travelled onwards to Wales, where the abandoned Cardiff Circus became the venue for a rousing two week mission. They progressed to the Midlands where the idea of using 'reformed sinners' to reform and recruit others was developed. William coined the phrase 'The Hallelujah Band' for these new crusaders. Although this initial band didn't last long after the Booth's departure back to London, the idea behind it took root in their minds.

The life of an itinerant preacher was hard. The lives of a man and wife, with a growing family at home to support, were plagued by financial worries. Catherine, being perhaps the more practical of the two, decided to try earning money by lecturing on temperance, a subject attracting a lot of interest. But "God's gypsies" – Catherine's own description – often struggled.

When Catherine was invited, in her own right, to preach to the Free Church Methodists at Rotherhithe, this marked a new phase in her life. William, unlike most Victorian husbands, encouraged her to take on a wider role. Her career as a preacher started to progress rapidly and her views on a range of matters, especially the living conditions of the poor, were becoming increasingly influential. She became involved in the work of an organization known as the Midnight Movement, devoted to the rescue and eventual redemption of prostitutes. And she was pregnant, again.

Then William was offered the chance to preach in the East End of London, initially in an old tent. He soon realized that there was much work to be done in the area, not just in converting his audiences but in keeping converts on the right path. As Frederick Booth-Tucker (Catherine's son-in-law) later commented, "It was a singular co-incidence that at the very time when Mr Booth was commencing his East End campaign, Mrs Booth was conducting her first West End services, so that the very antipodes of London were simultaneously assailed".

Catherine herself painted a very vivid picture in her *Reminiscences*, dictated in the last few months of her life. "He [William] went down to struggle with a continent of poverty, squalor, wretchedness, vice and crime, such as perhaps no city in the world has ever known before, while I was called to preach the salvation of God in the midst of wealth, pride, fashion and every imaginable form of luxury."

Catherine would raise money from her talks and preaching to

the rich to help with evangelical work amongst the poor; a pattern which was to continue for several years. Significantly, one of her sermons so impressed two trustees of the Bewley Fund, a charity working with London's poor, that they became involved in William's work in the East End. The charity funded the temporary hire of premises. And so the East London Christian Mission was born.

Catherine appears to have been concerned about the investment in property but, as Roy Hattersley argues, this was perhaps born out of her worries about the family's own financial circumstances. She had become the main breadwinner, even while carrying further additions to the Booth brood. But, as she had done all her life, she was prepared to put her trust in God – and in William.

Perhaps demonstrating a greater humility in old age than she had shown at the time, Catherine would recall in her final months how nervous she had felt speaking if William had been in the audience. Apparently, she had always felt that if he was present, it was he who should do the talking. If this was truly the case, then Catherine hid her feelings well. In reality, she appeared to revel in her ability to enthral an audience.

The influence and scope of the East London Christian Mission grew rapidly. The People's Market in Whitechapel was acquired and converted into the People's Mission Hall, with tea rooms, a shop and a soup kitchen. For both William and Catherine, tackling the effects, if not the causes, of poverty, had become an integral part of the evangelical work.

William spurned the approaches of patrons such as Henry Reed, who offered him greater financial security but only on condition that he worked exclusively at the East End Mission. As Catherine admitted in her *Reminiscences*, William and Henry Reed "were too much alike to work smoothly together for any considerable period". Once again, the Booths were looking further afield. Soon they were developing links and setting up new missions in other areas of the country.

William and Catherine were vociferous in their campaign against drinking and this led to some equally vociferous and sometimes violent attacks against them. Publicans didn't take kindly to the evangelists' habit of standing outside their licensed premises and distributing leaflets warning of the perils of drink. Some hired louts to attack them – another pattern which was to continue as their work spread.

"The time has come for Christians to denounce the use of intoxicating drinks as irreligious and immoral ... How can that which produces all this crime and misery be a good thing? And if it be an evil thing, how can it be moderately used?"

This quotation is from *Drinking Alcohol Versus Christianity*, one of Catherine Booth's *Papers on Practical Religion* printed in 1879. She had in fact delivered this paper at the Annual Conversazione of the National Temperance League in 1874. It was a theme she would hammer home to audiences at every opportunity.

Catherine had no time for the argument that the Bible permitted moderate drinking. In those "silvery, yet emphatic tones with which she commonly entered into such debates" she would declare that this was not her interpretation of the Bible. "If you read with care, you will observe that there are two kinds of wine referred to in the Bible, one intoxicating and the other not. The former is generally spoken of as 'strong drink', or some equivalent term, and is invariably coupled with language of condemnation, never used in connexion with the other."

Not surprisingly then, she also opposed the use of fermented wine in the communion service. "... banish it from His house. Put no longer the sacrifice of Christ and of devils on the same altar!"

The Booths were also anti-smoking and warnings about the perils of nicotine addiction featured in the journal of the Christian Mission.

The practice of using converts to preach to others was spreading.

Catherine did see some problems with this. For some of them "the sudden promotion from the taproom to the platform, with the applause and admiration of a listening crowd, without any sort of discipline, was more than many could bear, hence there were shipwrecks and disasters innumerable". Later she would urge the establishment of a training school, also providing continuing support for Salvationists. That notion of 'discipline' was always high on Catherine's agenda.

William was beginning to gather round him a group of influential, but perhaps rather eccentric, helpers but it was to Catherine that he listened most.

After reading William's tract *How to Reach the Masses*, a young evangelist, George Railton, became desperate to work with his hero. He joined the household, initially while working for the Mission on a trial basis. But his intellect and enthusiasm soon won over the Booths, who effectively adopted him. This must have been particularly difficult for their eldest son, Bramwell, reinforcing his anxiety that he could never live up to his parents' high expectations. For, despite his own health problems including hearing difficulties and depression, Bramwell had understood from an early age that he was expected to follow in his parents' footsteps.

Perhaps surprisingly, in the first few years of the Mission, Catherine spent much of the time concentrating her own evangelical efforts in places like Portsmouth, Hastings and Tunbridge Wells. She may not have been working alongside William, but she always made sure her audiences were aware of what was being achieved in London. As she moved on, she would often leave behind fledging branches of the Mission, helping extend its work and influence.

Like the 'Soldiers' Friend', Sarah Robinson, Catherine was shocked by the drunkenness and vice in port towns. She hired an old music hall at Southsea, a place surrounded by pubs and brothels and, perhaps even to her own surprise, started to attract audiences of 3,000 or more. Looking back at the end of her life, she recalled, "I had some wonderful times on that stage, times in which the Spirit of the Lord took possession of me." But she was also pleased that she had "no committee to control me". Discipline, it seemed, was alright for others.

As the Mission grew, military terminology crept in almost accidently. Some of the colourful evangelists recruited to the cause, such as George Railton and Elijah Cadman, seemed to relish the imagery of war. By 1877, the phrase 'Hallelujah Army' was frequently used in advertising for campaigns and rallies. This suited the personalities of both William and Catherine. They didn't feel they should be answerable to any committees, councils or conferences, only to God, but they also felt they were leaders, whose work was to bring the people to God.

Thus in 1878 The Salvation Army was created, a natural progression from the Mission. Uniforms and the famed 'Hallelujah bonnet', chosen by Catherine for its plainness and practicality, soon followed. Flags proclaimed the motto 'Blood and Fire'. There were no longer any geographical limitations in the organisation's name. But even William and Catherine couldn't have imagined that within 20 years, its work would spread around the globe.

Catherine was insistent that the rules of the new organisation allowed women to hold high rank and to have authority over men – something almost unheard of in Victorian times. Yet she herself never took a formal rank within the Salvation Army, preferring an "advisory rather than an executive" role.

Although the Mission had initially thrived on open air events, the Salvation Army began to acquire more and more premises, often without the necessary funds to pay for them. Catherine was bold in seeking financial and moral support. She wrote to Queen Victoria in one appeal. This elicited a response from the Queen's private secretary which Catherine had no hesitation in using in Salvation Army publicity. Apparently Her Majesty had learned "with great satisfaction that you have, with many members of your society, been successful in your efforts to win many thousands to the ways of temperance, virtue and religion". In fact, Queen Victoria made no financial contribution whatsoever to the appeal but her words, or those of her private secretary, contributed a great deal.

Bramwell's wedding, in 1882, provided a unique opportunity for fund-raising. Instead of being a private family celebration, the ceremony became more of a mass rally, with 6,000 Salvationists each paying one shilling admission – proceeds towards the purchase of the old Eagle Tavern, the Booths' latest project. The fact that father and mother both saw this as appropriate says much about their commitment to their work, which clearly took precedence over their family life.

As the Salvation Army grew, so did opposition and criticism. Salvation Army members were often arrested for nuisance and obstruction. Violence frequently ensued. Only Stead's *Pall Mall Gazette* drew attention to the fact that the police were often tacitly complicit in allowing mobs opposed to the Salvation Army to drive the evangelists from the streets.

Without doubt, one of the main flashpoints was the Army's opposition to the liquor trade. By 1880 all Salvation Army meetings closed with a plea for total abstinence. The voice of this populist movement, advocating teetotalism, could not be ignored. The brewers and the publicans feared for their livelihoods and provided money and free drink to those willing to disrupt Salvation Army gatherings. What became mockingly known as 'Skeleton Armies' were established in many small towns, funded by the breweries, with the specific aim of breaking up Salvation Army meetings.

Perhaps more surprisingly was the support given to these skeleton armies by some members of the established church, who feared that religion was being diluted by popularism. In 1880, the Bishop of Carlisle appeared, in a sermon, to support a drunken gang who had broken up a Salvation Army gathering in the city. It was Catherine Booth who hired a theatre in Carlisle to demonstrate the error of his ways – or his 'misunderstanding', as it was more charitably expressed. Her speech was subsequently published in the Army's *War Cry* magazine. It clearly set out the philosophy behind the Booths' style of evangelism. They were adapting not the message of the Gospel, but the way in which it was delivered – to "serve it up on any sort of dish that will induce the people to partake of it".

If marching bands, music hall tunes (with their lyrics changed to religious praise) and young 'Hallelujah Lasses' attracted audiences, this was perceived as an excellent way of reaching the people. Some of the 'Hallelujah Lasses' achieved their own fifteen minutes of fame. 'Happy Eliza' became such a celebrity that there were even dolls made in her likeness. Eliza had originally been sent up to Nottingham to inject some energy into a mission there. She caught the public imagination, marching through the town with her hair and clothes adorned with streamers, singing Salvationist songs at the top of her voice. When she moved back to London she travelled round Marylebone with her violin, attracting large audiences.

For a while civic authorities did all they could to avoid trouble. The easy way out was to ban all Salvation Army marches, something the Home Secretary seemed to be advocating. But the press, especially *The Times*, belatedly woke up to this threat to a basic liberty. For if an angry mob could stop Salvationists from passing along the highway, what else might they be able to stop if they so chose? Gradually the police provided greater protection against the agitators.

But there were still many violent incidents. Basingstoke in Hampshire witnessed some remarkable scenes. The town had at least 50 pubs and three breweries in 1880. When the Salvationists arrived in the town with the avowed intent of "opening fire on sin and Satan", the local brewers and publicans encouraged a motley gang, the Massagainians, to mock their efforts. The gang improvised their own instruments – saucepan lids, tin cans full of stones and fog horns – to drown out the sounds of the Salvation Army brass band. They followed them round the streets, intent on provoking a reaction. The town was split. Some town councillors marched with the Salvationists, others mixed with the Massagainians. Two petitions circulated. One, spearheaded by the local vicar, wanted the Salvation Army to stop their marches; the other, led by the local congregational church, wanted them to be allowed to march undisturbed. Tempers boiled over in March 1881, in the Battle of Church Square, as it became known. The Massagainians were inebriated, fuelled by free beer from the brewers. The Salvationists were jeered and shoved; one was rolled in the mud and ducked in the local stream. The Riot Act was read twice and the Royal Horse Artillery was sent in to disperse the 3,000 strong crowd which had gathered. Basingstoke hit the national headlines and questions were asked in Parliament.

A Salvation Army captain, Susannah Beaty, is regarded as the first Army 'martyr', killed by thugs in Hastings. She had been leading a procession through the streets and was pelted with rocks. One knocked her to the ground where she was kicked in the stomach; she later died from internal injuries.

In April 1882, during what might have been seen as the provocatively-titled 'Council of War' in Sheffield, William and Catherine both rode in an open carriage in a large procession. The Salvationists were attacked by a mob and several people were injured. But the marchers were so determined not to 'lose face' that even when Lieutenant Davidson, who was leading the procession, was knocked unconscious he was propped up on his horse as though all was well until the parade was over. It must have been a frightening experience, a strident reminder that, in challenging the liquor trade, the Salvation Army was fighting some very strong vested interests. Yet Catherine declared she was "so absorbed in the contemplation of the people that I seemed oblivious of any personal danger". Even when faced with a "hideous multitude" which seemed to be "thirsting for our very blood", Catherine still believed "we need to address their needs and bring them to God".

Major riots ensued along the south east coast, with Eastbourne, Hastings, Worthing and Brighton particular targets in 1884. On more than one occasion Dragoons from the real army had to be called in.

Some of the local presses, like *The Hastings & St Leonards Observer*, didn't actively support the Salvationists, referring to their "peculiar services". But they were forced to admit, as events unfolded, that the behaviour of the skeleton army was deplorable. Moreover, they reported, "two or three persons, from whose social position better things might have been expected, seemingly encouraging them". It wasn't quite a naming and shaming of local officials but it came close.

Similar incidents occurred throughout the country. There was always a scuffle to seize the Army flag, but the Salvationists became adept at protecting their standard, however much they were jeered and abused.

Catherine would have been heartened by the words of reformer, John Bright, who wrote to her saying, "The people who mob you would doubtless have mobbed the Apostles."

Once more the adage that all publicity is good publicity was proven. Due to the vocal and violent opposition, the work of the Salvation Army became more widely known. It was discussed in the highest circles and in the slums. Numbers swelled. The established church was forced to sit up and take notice. Members of Parliament, including Lord Shaftesbury, suddenly awoke to the potential of a vast, uniformed and disciplined body. It must have been with some relief that politicians came to see that the Salvation Army wasn't a potential threat to the country's stability but a driver for social change – a church of the people, for the people.

The Salvation Army worked with other temperance reformers throughout the world. Indeed, it was the American temperance leader, Frances Willard, who suggested Eveline Booth change her name to Evangeline. The Army also brought over half a million signatures to the Polyglot Petition which called on world leaders to stop promoting the liquor trade.

In the early 1880s there were even talks between the Church of England establishment and the Salvation Army about closer working relations. Catherine was actively involved in these discussions, which in themselves were a flattering acknowledgement of the Army's growing influence. Yet a union or amalgamation was never going to happen. Neither William nor Catherine would have been likely to accept the discipline of another church at this stage.

Further controversy followed as Catherine Booth and her son Bramwell became increasingly drawn into the work of Josephine Butler, herself a staunch teetotaller. Mrs Butler campaigned vociferously against the Contagious Diseases Act, which she believed effectively condoned prostitution whilst attempting to regulate it. Under the Act, prostitutes could be forced to undergo physical examinations and faced imprisonment if found to have venereal disease. Yet their male customers escaped any censure, seemingly absolved from any moral responsibility. Catherine and others had long realized that prostitutes needed help, not punishment. The establishment of refuges for these 'fallen women' became an important element of Salvation Army work.

Of particular concern was the increasing number of child prostitutes. Girls of just nine or ten might be 'sold' by their parents to work in brothels in major cities, even abroad. The Booths supported, even encouraged, journalist WT Stead to highlight this situation. And when Stead set up his 'purchase' of a young girl and wrote his series of articles *The Maiden Tribute of Modern Babylon* in *The Pall Mall Gazette*, the Salvation Army allowed it to be known that they had helped in the rescue of the young girl from moral danger and that she was safe in one of their homes in France. They argued that the case demonstrated the need for more Salvation Army Rescue Houses to be set up.

But WT Stead suddenly found himself on the wrong side of the law. In his haste and desire to expose child trafficking, he had only agreed the 'purchase' of the young girl in question with her mother and not her father. He was found guilty of abduction and assault and sent to prison. Bramwell Booth was also charged but acquitted on the basis that he had honestly believed the girl's mother was happy to leave her daughter in the care of the Salvation Army in France. This allowed the Army to distance itself from the affair, although Catherine did write to the Home Secretary begging for leniency for all the defendants.

In 1887, Catherine was diagnosed with breast cancer but refused surgery. She struggled on for over two years, still carrying out speaking engagements whenever she was well enough to travel. Her terminal illness didn't just have an emotional impact on her family and supporters; it brought with it a financial loss, as the collections after her sermons had brought in much needed funds to the Army's work.

Catherine managed to make a brief appearance at her husband's sixtieth birthday celebrations. Until she lost strength to do so, she wrote copious letters and tracts, many on the subject of temperance, and worked on her *Reminiscences*. When she could no longer write, she would dictate to a stenographer. Her death in October 1890 was marked by a military-style funeral. There was a grand parade with some 3,000 officers of the Salvation Army divided into 15 divisions, each separated by flags and banners.

Given that William's major work *In Darkest England and The Way Out* was published just two weeks after Catherine's death, it would seem likely that Catherine had a great influence on its major themes. Indeed the book was dedicated to her. It set out the Salvation Army's bold plans to rescue the outcasts of society. There would be city colonies – refuges providing basic necessities and temporary employment; farm colonies where people were taught to cultivate small holdings often in preparation for emigration and depots offering cheap, but not free, food. Each depot would hold Salvation meetings, providing a jovial, free and easy social evening – with prayer, addresses, testimonies and no alcohol. Whilst there was no compulsion for those using the depot to join in, the majority did so, thus facilitating an amazing growth in the Salvation Army's membership and influence.

Underpinning the ideas in the book was recognition that it was often social problems which made the working man turn to drink. Put in very simple terms, the philosophy was that alcohol consumption kept people away from God. If the Army could solve the social problems, it could solve the drink problems and so lead people to their salvation.

This philosophy was very much an echo of Catherine Booth's words in her paper *on Strong Drink Versus Christianity*. She argued that "total abstinence is a valuable ally of the gospel", valuable also "in separating men from those associations and habits which prevent them hearing the Gospel". She paints a powerful picture of the harm alcohol can do.

"The gambler seeks it [strong drink] to aid him in the craft and cunning by which he lures his victim on to financial ruin. The seducer has recourse to its deceptive power to pave the way for his cruel licentiousness. The burglar braces his courage and hardens his conscience by its exhilarating fumes. The harlot drowns in the intoxicating cup her sense of shame, and from it gathers strength to trample out the deepest, tenderest instincts of womanhood. The murderer is powerless to strike the fatal blow till maddened by its infernal stimulus."

In the context of this book, it is particularly interesting to look briefly at the achievements of William and Catherine's daughters. Even as a small child, Kate (christened Catherine after her mother) would often be brought on to the platform alongside her mother or father as a tactic to reduce heckling. In the nursery, Kate used to kneel her dolls at a carefully crafted penitent rail. She had clearly inherited much from her mother. She had also inherited her father's stubbornness and inability to mould personal views to fit established practice. Catherine actually refused Kate's desire for a formal education. By 17, Kate was preaching to adult audiences and appeared to have had no qualms in addressing noisy, hostile crowds. Before long she was leading an important element of the Salvation Army's work, working with 'fallen' women and setting up operations in France.

She married her second-in-command, Arthur Clibborn and became known as Catherine Booth-Clibborn. The couple had ten children. Yet in 1902, they resigned from the Salvation Army, having become frustrated by the organisation's discipline. They wanted to evangelise in their own way – as pacifists and advocates of faith-healing. Kate made it clear that supporting her husband in his beliefs meant more to her than the Salvation Army. This was heresy to her father. Kate became estranged from him and from the rest of the family. We can only speculate whether Catherine, had she still been alive at this juncture, would have been able to broker some reconciliation. She had clearly been very proud of Kate and had even made her one and only visit abroad to France when her daughter was leading Army operations there. But one suspects that Catherine would have put the Army, and William, before her daughter. It was Kate's defection which encouraged her brother Herbert to resign from the Salvation Army.

Emma initially took on the role of principal of the Salvation Army's first training home for women. She married Frederick Tucker, who had pioneered the Army's work in India and the couple worked there for several years before going to take over operations in America in 1896. Tragically, Emma died in a train accident in 1903, aged just 43.

Marion (Marie) suffered fits and had contracted smallpox as an infant but this hadn't prevented Catherine from leaving her when she was just five weeks old to go off preaching again. Marion never fully recovered. In her *Reminiscences*, Catherine described Marion as "in every way an invalid" yet she could apparently "apprehend and discharge the main duties of life and the all-important questions involved in her own salvation". It was clearly important to Catherine that Marion was still able to work with children, even if she couldn't cope with the rigours of high profile public preaching. She referred to Marion's disability as a "trial" – for her as a mother. She doesn't think to record what life was actually like for Marion herself. In later years, Marion was given the permanent rank of staff-captain, although she was unable to work regularly for the Army.

The fourth daughter, Eveline or Evangeline as she became known, was born in 1865 and went on to become General of the Salvation Army in 1934, having previously worked in London, Canada and, for 30 years, in America. She did much to develop the Army's role throughout the world yet she also took time to care for her sister Marion.

The youngest daughter, Lucy, worked for a while with her sister Emma in India and married Emmanuel Daniel Hellberg, a colonel in the Swedish Salvation Army. Together they worked in India, then in France and Switzerland. After she was widowed in 1909, Lucy

Banner of The British Women's Temperance Association
by kind permission of The White Ribbon Association (WTAEU)

Catherine Booth in Clacton on Sea 1889
by kind permission of The Salvation Army International
Heritage Centre

NBWTA Pledge card
by kind permission of The White Ribbon Association
(WTAEU)

Lady Henry Somerset
courtesy of Holmesdale Natural History Museum, Reigate

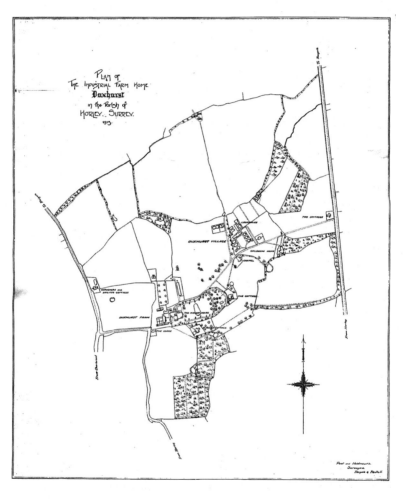

Duxhurst village
by kind permission of Reigate Priory Museum

Duxhurst cottages
courtesy of Arthur and Pauline Kennedy

Rosalind Howard
from the Castle Howard Collection, reproduced by kind
permission of the Hon. Simon Howard

Rosalind and George Howard and their family on the steps of Castle Howard from the Castle Howard Collection, reproduced by kind permission of the Hon. Simon Howard

continued with her Salvation Army work, serving as a territorial commander in Denmark, Norway and then South America.

So in many ways, Catherine and William were successful in their child-rearing. All their children, together with their partners, continued with evangelism and social reform around the world. Bramwell and Evangeline would in turn become Commander-in-Chief of the Salvation Army. They were all totally committed, as their parents had been, to doing God's work. But they couldn't all work together.

Whilst Catherine would undoubtedly have been proud of the work done by each of her children, she was spared the pain of seeing the family torn apart. In her final days, she urged all her children to "stand fast together". Did she foresee the trouble ahead? The military discipline which had enabled the Salvation Army to grow so fast and so furiously almost became its undoing.

Whilst William was busy travelling the world to see at first hand the work of his mighty organization, Bramwell, as Chief of Staff, decided to initiate a major reshuffle of his siblings. For example, Ballington was ordered back to England from America, Herbert was told to move from Canada to Australia, Evangeline from London to Canada, Kate from France to Holland. When they challenged Bramwell's authority, appealing to William that they hadn't been consulted, William backed his eldest son – not because he was the eldest but because he was Chief of Staff; as such his commands had to be obeyed. Had Catherine been alive, it is likely that she would have unreservedly endorsed William's attitude.

The result was that Ballington and his wife, Maud, resigned from the Salvation Army. Before long they had set up their own organisation, Volunteers of America, taking with them many of the original Salvationists. As we have seen, Kate, then Herbert, also broke away a few years later.

History has perhaps focused too much on the religious zeal of the Salvation Army and the practical help and support it gave, and still gives, to the poor. But Catherine's strong views on the religious rights of women were accepted and implemented by the Salvation Army. As Roy Hattersley comments, it effectively became "the first organization to prove that working women possessed the talent to lead".

The role of the Army, in particular the crusading passion of its 'mother', Catherine Booth, in promoting temperance in Victorian Britain deserves wider recognition. Undoubtedly, the lives of many working class people were touched and improved by Catherine and William Booth, their Salvation Army and those Hallelujah lasses.

Nor was the work just limited to Britain. For by Catherine's death, the Salvation Army was established in America, Australia, Africa, India and Europe, though not without some battles along the way.

Yet the Salvation Army proved strong enough to survive – an enduring legacy of a formidable couple.

Summarising Catherine's life is not easy. In many ways, she was admirable but not likeable. The powerful figure of William Booth is ever present in her story. Yet Catherine somehow managed both to hold her own place on the stage and to enhance the spotlight on her husband. She also ensured the show would go on long after her death.

CHAPTER 9

Lady Henry Somerset (1851 – 1921) and her Farm Colony for Inebriate Women

Although she had long been converted to the temperance cause and had taken the total abstinence pledge herself, Lady Henry Somerset (née Isabella Caroline Somers-Cocks) was initially reluctant to stand for President of The British Women's Temperance Association (BWTA) in 1889. She feared they wanted a mere titled figurehead, not a role she would find acceptable. She was also concerned that her earlier marital difficulties might bring the association into disrepute.

For by this stage of her life, Lady Henry had suffered social humiliation. She had dared to challenge her husband for the custody of their young son and accused him of what was then a crime – homosexuality. She may have gained her judicial separation and even won custody of the child, but it was she who was then shunned by society.

But this experience was to give Lady Henry a unique empathy with others, including those brought low by drug or alcohol abuse. She was very non-judgmental. She knew from her own experience that outward appearances often disguised a different truth; that people were not always the architects of their own fall from grace. We need, she said, to put "ourselves exactly in their position, to realize how easily the same thing might have happened to us, how between us and the man who has lost his social footing there is no real gulf, only a false step which we ourselves might have taken" – an unusual recognition from a lady of high birth.

Isabel, as she was known, was the eldest daughter of Charles, Lord (later 3rd Earl) Somers and his wife Virginia, a renowned and well-connected beauty. The family's estates included glorious swathes of Herefordshire, Worcestershire and Gloucestershire, with the imposing Eastnor Castle at their centre. They also owned most of the town of Reigate in Surrey, with Reigate Priory a useful country home conveniently close to London. Less salubrious were the estates of Somers Town in the St Pancras area of London where overcrowding was high and sanitation standards low.

With no son to inherit the estates, her parents were keen for Isabel to make a good match. She had led a very sheltered childhood, stifled, she felt, by a procession of governesses who sought to curb her natural spirit. Her father was not over impressed by the suit of Lord Henry Somerset. As second son of the Duke of Beaufort, he had a title but no money. Her mother however was most impressed by the title and helped persuade her somewhat reluctant daughter to accept Lord Henry's proposal.

Sadly, the marriage went wrong from the very first days of the honeymoon. Lord Henry told his astonished bride that he wished them to lead separate lives. Although the couple did have a son, Lord Henry made it clear there would be no more.

To the outside world, Isabel put on a brave face. Behind the scenes her parents and her parents-in-law were concerned; the Somers for the welfare of their daughter and grandson; the Beauforts perhaps more for the family's reputation. It was only when she discovered correspondence between her husband and his male friends that Isabel finally understood the reality of her domestic situation.

Perhaps some Victorian ladies would have merely turned a blind eye to their husband's behaviour. That was the custom of the day in the higher echelons of society. But Isabel wasn't prepared to do so. Confrontation was inevitable. It came one evening when they were staying at their London home. Isabel was dining with her parents at a near-by hotel. Word came via a servant that her husband and one of his friends had paid a visit to their son's nursery, watching the boy as he slept. Isabel was shocked and feared for her son's safety. Her parents advised her to have the child brought immediately to the hotel, into their safe keeping. Isabel sent a message to the nurse to bring the boy straight round. With the child safely settled at the hotel, she bravely returned to the marital home.

Lord Henry reacted angrily, threatening a writ of *Habeas Corpus* to have the child returned to his custody. He rushed round to the hotel to confront his parents-in-law. "Child-stealers", he called them. As he returned to the house, Lady Somers sent her butler to bring Isabel to the hotel. They felt it was no longer safe for her to stay in the house with her husband. Isabel later described the sorry state she was in: wearing her dressing gown, hair down, one slipper on, one slipper off. Not a dignified exit from what should have been a glittering marriage.

Despite the attempts of friends and family to broker a settlement (even Disraeli got involved urging Lady Somers to avoid a scandal which would distress the Queen), the case went to court, in May 1878. The judge, Mr Justice Field, having heard all the arguments, gave his verdict. We must bear in mind the law and moral code of the day, remember that this occurred before the celebrated trial of Oscar Wilde and be grateful that attitudes have now changed. The judge declared there wasn't sufficient evidence to find Lord Henry guilty of the "heinous crime" of which he had been accused but that there was sufficient evidence to show that he had effectively forced his wife from the marital home. Thus he granted Isabel a judicial separation and, most tellingly, he granted her custody of their son. At a time when a father's rights were deemed paramount, this was an unusual step.

Her husband actually continued in his role as MP and

Comptroller of the Queen's household for another year before he decided it was prudent to go and live abroad. His life too had been irrevocably damaged by his marriage and the attitudes of the day.

Although in years to come she would be fêted on both sides of the Atlantic, Isabel never forgot her grief, guilt and shame at her failed marriage. For several years she lived quietly at Reigate Priory, no longer welcome at court, shunned even by her own sister's mother-in-law, the Duchess of Bedford. She enjoyed spending time with her son and modestly entertaining the few friends who had remained faithful to her. Slowly the truth about her unhappy marriage became more widely known. But she had been scarred by the aristocracy's treatment of her.

Isabel started to take an interest in the welfare of the family's tenants in Reigate. She became aware that many young girls were leaving the local workhouse with no place to go, untrained for domestic service of any type. Unsurprisingly some of them ended up on the streets. So, in 1884, she set up St Mary's Home to take in such girls and train them as laundry maids.

In mid-Victorian England, it wasn't unusual for the ladies of the manor to become involved in charitable projects. What was unusual was Isabel's dedication to making things better for women and children in practical ways, giving of herself and her talents. At times, this even meant stripping the sheets from her own bed to give to a family in need. Isabel took in a young cousin, Laura Gurney, who had been orphaned. Laura was soon encouraged to help out running Sunday School at St Mary's. She was well placed to witness what she described as Isabel's "human sympathy" and noted, "... she projected herself, so to speak into the whole question of the trouble ... and showed a vivid burning interest betrayed in countless quick questions, after which she would think it over in silence for a moment, then there would be definite action of some sort."

Running a home like St Mary's was expensive and Isabel didn't have unlimited access to the family money. On her father's death in October 1883, the estates had been tied up to be inherited by a male cousin, and trustees watched over her shoulder at all times. She had a personal allowance and use of the family properties during her lifetime. So she put her talents as an author and watercolourist to good effect and produced a charming book of children's verse, *Our Village Life*, which was sold to raise money for the project.

Soon after her father died, Isabel decided she needed to make Eastnor Castle her main home but her social conscience had now been awakened. Within a few miles of the grandeur of Eastnor she found life was harsher. Whilst today Ledbury is a charming market town, with beautiful timbered buildings, in the 1880s it was a grim place – awash with alcohol-fuelled squalor.

Isabel started going out in the evenings with a local Methodist woman, Mrs Ridley, visiting the sick and poor. Some people were suspicious of her motives. Isabel just wanted to help. And in helping others, she found she was helping herself to cope with the grief of her failed marriage. Nothing was more comforting than the uncomplicated trust of a child. In her diary (sadly now lost but quoted in Kathleen Fitzpatrick's 1923 biography), Isabel wrote about how she came across two young girls one night. They came from a family of ten and their mother had just died. She went straightaway with them to console the father. "I wonder if they could ever believe the comfort they brought to my heart when they each stole a little hand into mine …"

Religion had always been important to Isabel and her faith was strengthened by an experience she later recounted. Sitting under a tree in Reigate Priory Park, she was musing on the meaning of life. Was God real? She heard a voice, coming as though from deep within herself, saying "Act as if I am and thou shalt know I am."

Isabel believed God should be accessible to all. She had no time for clergy who only welcomed the middle and upper classes in their

'Sunday Best'. It was a view which brought her into conflict with some of the local clergy around Eastnor. They certainly didn't approve of the tin tabernacles or mission huts she had erected in the surrounding villages. One year, they even went so far as to boycott her annual tea party at Eastnor, sending no apology or explanation. Isabel merely invited the local cricket club along to enjoy the hospitality which had been prepared. Rising above the insult, the following year Isabel invited the clergy as usual. This time they did attend, their earlier petty protest studiously ignored by all.

Isabel set up a Mission Hall in Bye Street, Ledbury, amongst all the public houses. Classes, mothers' meetings and clothing clubs were established. She preached herself, joining itinerant missions travelling the country. She even preached in the blackness of the pits in South Wales – an experience which she later said stood her in good stead when addressing huge audiences in grand halls in America. Isabel was a fine orator. She always found a way to tug at the heart strings. But her rhetoric was always reinforced by hard facts. She could quote statistics about the number of public houses and the number of arrests linked to drunkenness. She displayed a real knowledge of real people because she took the time to see how they lived, making her words even more powerful.

Her friend and neighbour, Lady Elizabeth Biddulph, introduced Isabel to the temperance cause and persuaded her to join the Ledbury branch of The British Women's Temperance Association (BWTA). The Association had been growly slowly since being founded in 1876. It did a lot of good work, especially at a local level but at this stage it was not a major force in temperance politics.

Realising that so many of the problems she saw in the streets of Ledbury were either cause, or effect, of excessive drinking, Isabel set up a small temperance society at Eastnor for her tenants. And, of course, this meant she had to lead by example. She signed the pledge at her Eastnor society's first meeting. This meant giving up the moderate drinking which she had hitherto enjoyed. She told friends later how, on her way back from London to attend that meeting at Eastnor, she had had to change trains at Worcester. She couldn't resist the lure of the station refreshment room or the taste of one last glass of port. She was a very human heroine.

In fact Isabel really believed that moderation, not prohibition, was the answer. In 1889, over a century before the Human Rights Act, she declared, "I maintain that no Government has a right to make arbitrary laws to enforce sobriety, as that is a system which would only impair the liberty of the nation." Significantly she added, "But every good government can make it easy to do right, and difficult to do wrong."

These words were spoken on New Year's Day, 1889, when Isabel was initiated into the Independent Order of Rechabites at Hereford. The Rechabites were a Friendly Society which had been founded in 1835 and which had built up a wide network of branches, spreading the cause of temperance. Their name came from a tribe of abstainers in The Old Testament. Isabel was privileged to be welcomed into the Rechabites. It was unusual for them to accept women as full members in their own right, although the branches organized many family activities as alternatives to socializing in the pubs.

In her inaugural speech to the Rechabites, Isabel spoke of the "great tide of misery" springing from the two mighty rivers of "Intemperance" and "Improvidence". She referred to the human cost, and the financial cost, of the problems caused by excessive drinking. "We are buying dearly all the evils that strong drink is producing."

Later in 1889, Isabel was elected to the presidency of the BWTA. She made it clear, in no uncertain terms, that she would not just be that 'titled figurehead'. She had grand plans, many of them based upon ideas coming across the Atlantic. She wanted departments within the BWTA, each working on different social problems of the day – poverty, children's welfare, women's suffrage, prison reform, to name but a few. She felt that the Association, which attracted women from all classes of society, had the potential to be so much more than a lobbying group against the liquor trade. She set up a press department, with a view ultimately to having her own journal, to promote the work of the BWTA. She even funded many of these activities herself, paying all her own expenses as she travelled the length and breadth of the country on BWTA business.

Isabel was soon to discover that women's temperance politics were both dirty and divided. Many of the executive council members wanted to press for prohibition, many more wanted to focus just on the temperance issue. The latter group was not interested in all the other 'causes' which Isabel chose to adopt. Or, even if they were interested, they preferred to join other societies campaigning on that particular issue. The 'Do-Everything' policy of the Americans was anathema to the old guard.

Stories soon started appearing in the press about where Isabel's money came from. For, amongst their large estates, the Somers family owned pubs and even a brewery. Isabel fought many a battle to have some of these closed down. Near the gates of Eastnor Castle, the old Somers Arms became a temperance hotel. But the trustees of her father's estate often blocked her wishes. When she tried to stop the licence of a Reigate inn being renewed, the trustees took her to court to prevent this. De-licensing meant a reduction in the estate's income. For the family this was far more important than Isabel's principles.

Isabel was greatly influenced by an American Quaker, Mrs Hannah Whitall Smith, who had settled in England and become involved with the BWTA. Hannah saw Isabel as her protégée. She also recognized that Isabel had much in common with the American temperance leader, Frances Willard. She determined that the two should meet. In the circular letters which Hannah sent back to her friends in America (now preserved at the Lilly Library in the Indiana University of America and quoted in Olwen Niessen's academic study *Aristocracy, Temperance and Social Reform – the Life of Lady Henry Somerset*) she extolled the virtues of her two dear friends. She took great delight in the friendship which developed between them. She seemed to know instinctively that Isabel and Frances would be a powerful coalition. The next few years were to prove how right this instinct was.

With Hannah's encouragement, Isabel was determined to travel to the States; ostensibly to attend the Boston convention of the World Woman's Christian Temperance Union (WWCTU), but most importantly to meet Frances Willard, founder of that body. In 1891, Hannah and Isabel travelled across the Atlantic on the luxury steamship Teutonic. At this point in her life, Isabel was still very much the aristocratic lady. She enjoyed the fine trappings of the ship's state rooms and no doubt made use of its extensive library. When Hannah became sea-sick, Isabel knew exactly the right cure – iced champagne – purely for medicinal purposes of course!

As an aristocrat, Isabel could be sure of a warm welcome in America; a private reception with the President, an audience of 3,000 in Washington. America started to fall in love with the attractive, articulate 'English Lady'. Isabel was invited to stay at Frances Willard's modest home in Evanston, Illinois, prior to the main convention. Sometimes eagerly anticipated meetings fail to live up to expectations. Not this one. There was an immediate bonding. Frances described Isabel as "unassuming, cordial, delightful"; Isabel thought Frances "far nicer and lovelier than she had ever dreamed".

The two women addressed meetings in Chicago. Over 2,000 people had to be turned away from the city's concert hall; 4,000 crowded in. The press fawned over Isabel. But all this was a prelude to the massive WWCTU Convention assembled in Boston. People had come from all corners of the globe – Japan, Australia, South

Africa, China, Italy. Religious organizations of all denominations were present, including the Salvation Army now well established in America. "Baptists, Quakers, Methodists, Unitarians, Episcopal Church, Presbyterians, all in perfect harmony, all taking part, and a spirit in the immense meetings of healthy, breezy, progressiveness and God's spirit brooding over all," Isabel wrote, clearly enchanted and inspired by the occasion.. She was elected vice-president-at-large, with Frances the president of the Union.

Frances Willard was a third-generation American, from a deeply religious family. Her mother in particular was a great influence on her. Frances never married, having broken off an engagement to a friend of her brothers. At the time, and in the many biographies written about her after her death, religious differences were cited as the reason for the break-up. It is only now, thanks to the work of Carolyn De Swarte Gifford who has transcribed Frances' private journal, that we know the truth. Frances felt "tormented with the abnormal love and longing of a woman for a woman".

Frances started as a teacher but soon became increasingly involved in campaigning for women's issues – not just suffrage but women's religious and economic rights and temperance. Frances saw excessive drinking as the root of many social problems and became a staunch prohibitionist. On one occasion, she joined the 'Crusade' women in Pittsburgh, falling on her knees outside a bar praying for the owner to renounce his trade.

Like Isabel Somerset, Frances was a prolific writer, a commanding orator and a superb organizer. By 1879, Frances had become President of the American Woman's Christian Temperance Union (WCTU), having served as president of the Chicago branch, then as secretary of the national Union.

Carolyn De Swarte Gifford describes the WCTU under Frances's stewardship as "a powerful vehicle for women's self-development ... a kind of school to train women for responsible participation in the public life of their country." It might also have been described as a breeding ground for feminists. Yet Frances remained a "womanly woman". De Swarte Gifford describes her demeanour as "a welcome alternative to what [the American public] perceived as the strident, demanding stance of more radical women's rights leaders".

Frances was also keen to unite women's reform movements around the world. So in 1884 she had formed the World Woman's Christian Temperance Union (WWCTU), with its 'Do-Everything' policy. Women were exhorted to fight "For God and Home and Everyland" against all social ills, not just the widespread abuse of alcohol. Frances believed women should have the vote; women would clean up politics and "make the world home-like". This was an exact mirror of Isabel Somerset's views.

Isabel made the most of her first visit to the States. As well as parties and receptions, she took time to witness the seedier side of life across the ocean. Wisely accompanied by two detectives, effectively bodyguards, she visited "the dives of New York" to see the opium dens. She also went to the Sing Sing Convict prison and "cried like a child" at what she saw there. She went to Minneapolis to help set up the Rest Island Mission for Intemperate Men.

Isabel found it hard to leave America and her new friends, especially Frances. She extended her visit and enrolled at the famous Dwight Moody School, taking bible classes and receiving training in evangelical work. After a day of study, she, with her fellow students, went out into the streets to put their training into practice.

Together with Frances, Isabel took an active role in editing the *Union Signal*, the official journal of the Woman's Christian Temperance Union. Editing involved writing many articles herself. Isabel absorbed all these experiences like a sponge. They would inspire and assist her future work in Britain, especially when in 1893 she bought *The Woman's Herald* (formerly *The Women's Penny Paper*) to promote not just temperance matters but all women's issues including suffrage and social reform.

On her return to England, Isabel found that her popularity amongst the executive committee of the BWTA had diminished because of her lengthy stay in America. Yet her standing and popularity with the grass roots of the women's temperance movement became even greater. Her desire to make women's suffrage an integral part of the Association's work was a real stumbling block. Isabel was not, in fact, a suffragette. She was a suffragist, believing that the argument for women's right to vote should be made by legal means and rational debate, not grand gestures of open defiance.

Isabel had the courage and energy to fight her detractors. Over the next few years she used every means at her disposal. Her great skills as an orator and writer were put to the test.

Over the next few years, a pattern developed. Isabel would make long trips to America. Frances would come to England. Although neither woman enjoyed robust health, they were constantly working for their various causes, including promoting the Polyglot Petition calling on all world leaders to stop encouraging the liquor trade. Frances had originally launched this petition in 1885 but with Isabel's help, it became a huge publicity exercise. For several years it was taken around the world by WWCTU missionaries. Isabel paid for two bound volumes to be printed with the petition's text and photographs of all the 178,095 signatures of the British women. These were then presented to Queen Victoria. Although the petition was presented to many of the 'Governments of the World' to whom it was addressed, it had little influence on their policies.

Isabel and Frances travelled widely. They wrote, they lectured, they preached. Even when on a cycling holiday in France, they detoured to Marseilles to spearhead an operation to help Armenian refugees fleeing the invading Turks. Some of the refugees came to

England, enjoying a short stay at Reigate Priory before being found homes and positions. The majority, however, were encouraged to emigrate to America, with Frances and Isabel using all their contacts to expedite the process.

WT Stead, in a glowing character sketch in *The Pall Mall Gazette*, made the perceptive comment that Isabel might fare better if she didn't get involved in so many causes. Her health, and her wealth, was suffering.

Each year, the BWTA's annual conference was beset with arguments. In 1893, the inevitable happened. Before the conference, Isabel circulated a paper, *Outline of the Progressive Policy*, to all the BWTA affiliated branches, together with a work plan for the following year. She omitted reference to the fight for women's suffrage in the hope this would pacify some of her colleagues. It didn't. They circulated their own paper, demonstrating their desire to focus efforts on lobbying for restrictions to the drink trade. It was decided to hold a pre-conference meeting to try to sort out the differences. Isabel objected to the proposed chairman – a man – on the basis that the women should be capable of sorting out their own problems. The National Executive Committee then abandoned the idea of the pre-meeting. Then they resurrected it, notifying all the branches, but somehow neglecting to tell their own president. Isabel was appalled when she found out, but refused to attend.

At the subsequent annual conference, Isabel went on the attack. She needed no lessons in political manoeuvring. She arranged for her speech to be printed and then given out to delegates just as she began to talk. She was not giving her opponents the benefit of advanced warning. But she did allow some of her irritation to show through saying, "perhaps no-one in the association has relinquished more of leisure and opportunity of pleasure and ease … than I have put aside to join the ranks of those who march along the dusty highway of a reformer's life." This was a rare public indication that

Isabel did realise she could have chosen an easier life. In private, as diary extracts show, she chastised herself for being interested in fashion or the theatre. She was her own harshest critic.

Most of the delegates cheered and applauded. It was well into the evening before the final votes were counted, but Isabel had won the day. The defeated committee members, who termed themselves the 'majority' on the executive, resigned to start up their own organization, the Women's Total Abstinence Union (WTAU). Some thirty three years later, in 1926, the two groupings amalgamated once more under the banner National British Women's Total Abstinence Union.

So in 1893, the BWTA became the National British Women's Temperance Association (NBWTA), with Isabel at its helm; an Isabel who now had a mandate for a full reforming agenda. At last she could have her desired specialist departments to work on issues such as suffrage, prison and police court work, social purity and prevention of cruelty to children. She also encouraged the NBWTA to become involved in labour issues such as relief work for the families of striking miners.

A massive demonstration was held in Hyde Park in support of the Direct Veto Bill, which would give power to local authorities to grant, renew or refuse liquor licences in their own area. Isabel led the NBWTA contingent, driving around London for four hours in a horse drawn carriage decorated with blue and white flowers – the Association's colours. The bill wasn't passed by Parliament but this didn't stop Isabel campaigning for changes which would curtail the drink trade.

The BWTA had for a while been running a small home in Sydenham for women recovering from alcohol problems. This home passed to the newly formed WTAU. This might have been a blow to some, but for Isabel it was an opportunity. It meant she could pursue her plans for a whole village to be devoted to the care of women of all classes who had fallen prey to alcoholism.

Isabel had always read widely and made sure she took the opinion of experts in their field. Thus she was aware of the work done by Pastor von Brodelschwing and his village homes for people with epilepsy. It occurred to her that alcoholism could be treated in the same way. When one of her colleagues, Dr Sarah Anderson, proposed the idea of a farm colony, Isabel was immediately interested. Dr Anderson had been studying methods of treatment in various parts of the world, including Germany and America. She had seen how direct contact with nature could deliver some amazing results for patients.

Isabel could ill afford to buy land for such a scheme but in 1894 she went ahead with the purchase of the Duxhurst estate, just a few miles south of her Reigate home, on a long lease from Christ's Hospital. From the very beginning the NBWTA refused to take on financial responsibility for the project, although the Association did help in fundraising and happily took credit for some of its early achievements. Isabel herself bore the managerial responsibility as well as the financial burden.

There was already a manor house on the estate. This was a great attraction to Isabel – not for herself but because she could use this to get the project up and running very quickly. The manor house would be used for the rehabilitation of the rich and famous of the day, the aristocratic ladies, opera singers and music hall stars who had fallen into alcohol or drug abuse. These ladies could pay for their care and accommodation. The Duxhurst manor house was effectively the 'Priory clinic' of the late Victorian period.

There was also a separate house, Hope Cottage, on the fringes of the estate which Isabel deemed suitable for middle class women who could afford to pay something towards their keep. But what of the poor working class women or those who had been in and out of prison because they couldn't find any way to escape their drunken habits? For them, Isabel designed small thatched cottages around a village green. What a contrast it must have been to their former homes – green fields, good food and not a public house in sight!

Each cottage housed six or eight women, under the care of a House Sister. These House Sisters were usually recruited from The Church Army and great care was taken to match the temperament of the Sister with the women in her care. Meals were taken in the main hall, at the top end of the green.

Making use of her status and connections, Isabel was able to attract Mary, Duchess of Teck to perform the official opening of the village in 1896. In the same year, she also showed off the project to the women of the WWCTU, in London for their second biennial conference. Being Isabel, each occasion was a means to raise both profile and funds. Over the years, Duxhurst was a major source of financial strain and, by her own admission, Isabel was not good with money.

Isabel's philosophy was that fresh air and exercise were good for everyone. So Duxhurst had gardens, orchards, lavender fields, greenhouses, even a small dairy farm at one point. Laundry and sewing were done outside whenever possible although there were also laundry buildings and several workshops on site. In one such workshop, huge looms were installed. The women produced some wonderful embroidered items which were then sold in shops such as Selfridges. There was even a pottery. Isabel herself was very artistically talented; she could write, paint, sculpt and sew. Such activities brought her pleasure. So she believed they would help the women of Duxhurst. "The moral effect of being able to create something of beauty is curiously apparent," Isabel wrote.

Isabel had her own house built at Duxhurst, modestly named 'The Cottage'. This is one of the few buildings to survive today. The thatched cottages around the green have long disappeared, as also has the beautiful church which Isabel established there. St Mary and the Angels was initially very small and very simple. It was dedicated in 1896 in a special service led by Canon Wilberforce of Westminster, a keen temperance supporter and friend to Isabel.

Over the years the church became more ornate and had several extensions. Roses grew both outside and within. Wonderful ornaments were collected by Isabel on her travels abroad to adorn the church. The doors were always open, providing a place for quiet contemplation. A small graveyard was established at the side of the church; a few remnants of graves can still be found today, amongst the tangled scrub which now pervades much of the area.

As Isabel's religious leanings became ever more High Anglican, much religious imagery found a home at Duxhurst, including a large Calvary cross. The NBWTA objected but Isabel always insisted the village was non-denominational. She did not insist patients attended church at Duxhurst, she merely made the church such an integral part of the village community that sooner or later most women felt drawn to find inner peace and heal themselves by accepting God into their life. Quiet conversions were the norm at Duxhurst, not the high drama of open air missions, such as those supported by the Salvation Army. Yet Isabel admired Catherine Booth and actually stated on several occasions that she would have been very happy as a Hallelujah lass, in her bonnet, visiting the sick and lonely. She also worked closely with the Salvation Army to facilitate the emigration of women from Duxhurst to America or Canada, to start new lives.

Another key feature of Duxhurst was the presence of children. Initially 'The Nest' had been built as a holiday home for children from the slums, where they could enjoy a week's respite from their squalid living conditions. But Isabel soon realized that there were many children who suffered greatly at the hands of alcoholic parents – battered, abused and neglected. So The Nest became a permanent children's home offering a place of safety, love and the simple pleasures of country life.

Isabel had long realized that alcoholism was not just the curse of the poor. One of her own aristocratic friends had committed suicide after falling victim to alcoholism. She knew drug use, especially opium smoking, was rife in all sectors of society. "It is shameful the ease with which drugs are obtained," she commented. She was appalled that laudanum, a tincture of opium, was given to children. It might keep them quiet but, in her view, it slowly killed them.

At Duxhurst, Isabel succeeded in breaking down class barriers. She often claimed that the gardens, the children and the church were all instrumental in this. But her own personality, non-judgmental attitude and what Chekhov called her "talent for humanity" also played a major part.

Isabel once again put her writing talents to good use to produce a book about her work at Duxhurst. *Beauty for Ashes,* published in 1913, was unashamedly a fund-raising effort, designed to show the excellent work being done at the village. We must therefore expect a certain poetic licence in the statistics given about success rates – 73% of those who stayed for over a year – especially as Isabel was adept at excluding many categories of patients e.g. the insane, the criminal or those whom we would now describe as having learning difficulties.

The authorities were very impressed with the work done at Duxhurst. For financial reasons, Isabel allowed two of the Duxhurst cottages to be registered under the Inebriates Act but she clearly regretted this. Women responded much better if they had come to Duxhurst voluntarily, she claimed. Referrals always outnumbered the places available. In one year alone, there were 3,200 applications for just 50 places.

Isabel had a close working relationship with a Police Court Missionary, Thomas Holmes, who frequently interceded with judges to refer the accused to Duxhurst, not prison. Isabel wasn't above going to the courts herself if she was aware of a special case. This is how the notorious Jane Cakebread, a veteran of almost 300 jail sentences, came to Duxhurst. Sadly for all concerned, she was not one of Isabel's successes and lasted just three difficult months there. Isabel later described Jane as "in no ordinary sense an inebriate. She was an insane woman who became dangerously violent when drunk".

Jane was ultimately admitted to an asylum and an article in *The Pall Mall Gazette* blamed this fact on Isabel's "mischievous interference". Such a slur on the work at Duxhurst could not go unchallenged. Isabel sued for libel and won!

In her own book, *Beauty for Ashes*, Isabel contrasts the insanity of Jane Cakebread with the behaviour of another patient at Duxhurst, Annie Adams. Like Jane, Annie had been in prison many times. But unlike Jane, Annie was "pathetically tractable" when sober. As Isabel put it, Annie was "a sane person who had been constantly overcome by the effects of alcohol, but whose mind regained its balance under normal conditions".

Through her work and research, Isabel became a leading expert in the treatment of women with alcohol and drug problems. She made a great study of the causes of alcoholism. She acknowledged that for many women there was a 'last straw', something which "broke her spirit, when her body was already past breaking-point". A typical woman at Duxhurst would have had a history of "over-work, insufficient nourishment during child-bearing, ill-health as a result, and subsequent break-down".

She didn't think it was the taste of the alcoholic drink which was the attraction for alcoholics. If it was, they wouldn't be prepared to drink methylated spirit or lamp paraffin, she argued. What they craved was "a sensation, a stimulation, or a soporific … that, having once experienced, they desire to experience again and again".

Whilst those who had not succumbed to alcoholism might be

able to drink moderately, the only cure for the alcoholic was total abstinence, in Isabel's opinion. She became quite incensed that many tonics and medicines contained alcohol, unbeknown to many people. This could, and did, cause some who had been cured of their addiction to fall prey to it again.

Under Isabel's presidency, the NBWTA supported the National Temperance Hospital which had been set up near Euston, where alcohol could only be prescribed in exceptional circumstances. They sponsored a bed in the women's surgical ward, donating £1,000 to dedicate it 'in loving memory of Margaret Bright Lucas', Isabel's predecessor as president of the association.

When a Royal Commission on Liquor Licensing Laws was set up in 1897, the NBWTA lobbied, unsuccessfully, to have women appointed to the group. Some of the male-dominated temperance associations had been included. At least Isabel, in her role as President of the NBWTA, was invited to give evidence. As usual, she did her research, supporting all her points with solid evidence. She recognized the vested interests of the liquor trade. She understood that magistrates were loathe to reduce the number of licences in their area because this meant a loss of income for the licence holder. Her favoured solution, one she did feel was practicable, was reform with compensation. So if a licence was not renewed, the licence holder should be paid compensation which would be met by contributions from the remaining licensees in the area. In addition, each area should have the right of 'direct veto', so that public opinion was given influence in deciding how many licensed premises there should be in their vicinity.

Isabel had remained constant to the views she had expressed in her initiation speech to the Rechabites in 1899. She still believed there was nothing inherently wrong in moderate drinking for most people. She did not believe in prohibition, partly because she felt it would be "absolutely impracticable" at that time. But these views, when expressed to the Commission, were deemed heretical by some of her colleagues in Britain.

"Q. Do you think that simply drinking by itself is wrong?
"A. No, I cannot say that I do.

"Q. May I assume that if there were no such thing as immoderate drinking there would be no need for any of the organizations with which you are connected?
"A. None whatever.

"Q. You would not wish that men should be made teetotalers by Act of Parliament?
"A. No, I should not believe in it.

"Q. Therefore I may say you are not in favour of prohibition?
"A. I should certainly not be in favour of Prohibition by Act of Parliament. I think I should be in favour of such education that it would lead to an inanition of the trade."

Isabel's evidence was credited with persuading Lord Peel, Chairman of the Commission, that licensing reform was necessary.

However, mirroring the conflict both with the liquor trade and amongst the temperance reformers themselves, the Commission was unable to reach a unanimous conclusion. Both minority and majority reports were produced. Whilst both reports accepted the need for a reduction in the number of licences, the majority thought this should be done gradually, with generous compensation for those affected. The minority, headed by Lord Peel, wanted a swifter reduction in the number of licences and compensation restricted to seven years, with direct veto to be gradually introduced in Scotland and Wales, deferred indefinitely in England.

Isabel knew that while the temperance movement was divided, it would be ineffective politically. Like many she deemed the majority report as favourable to the trade. She realized the minority report recommendations, whilst not all the NBWTA wanted, were the best they could hope for. She urged all the factions to work together, "to work for measures upon which they could agree, even though they might not be all they might ultimately hope to secure". She persuaded the Association to back Lord Peel and the Liberals at the forthcoming election. Despite the Liberals' subsequent defeat by the Tories, the NBWTA continued to back the minority proposals.

Another idea which Isabel was keen to promote was that favoured by Joseph Rowntree and Arthur Sherwell, known as 'disinterested management'. The theory was that if publicans became salaried employees, then they would have no personal vested interest in pushing sales, especially to people who clearly had already over-imbibed.

Isabel's pragmatism caused her problems in other areas. In 1897, she upset many, especially amongst the ranks of the World's Union including her friend Frances Willard, by supporting proposals for a form of state regulation of prostitution in India. Her objectives, as usual, centred on the welfare of innocent women and children, the families of military men who had contracted venereal disease from visiting prostitutes whilst overseas.

Isabel did not support any 'dual standard', a system which punished the prostitutes themselves, whilst allowing their male customers to go uncensored. But clearly something needed to be done. Her practical proposals, published in an open letter to Lord Hamilton, raised a furore on both sides of the Atlantic. Even though Isabel had made it clear that she was stating her personal views and not representing any formal body, she was denounced by many of her NBWTA colleagues. Isabel had betrayed her sex, they cried.

Women like Josephine Butler, once a friend, became bitter enemies. Questions were asked – was Isabel fit to be the WWCTU's Vice President? The venom which rained down on Isabel was extraordinary and some letters written and received by her at the time show how much hurt this caused her. Yet her proposals were supported by many notable women including the Duchess of Teck and Florence Nightingale, and some newspaper editors lauded her as the 'saviour' of English women's reputation.

Despite their close friendship, Frances Willard found it difficult to defend Isabel on this issue. But Frances was also unwilling to condemn Isabel outright, so she too was accused of treachery. Eventually, feeling she had been greatly misunderstood and probably feeling she was contributing to Frances' ill-health, Isabel publically recanted her proposals.

Sadly, Frances died in February 1898 at the age of just 58. Her last months were a battle to get as much work done as possible whilst resting and undergoing various medical treatments whenever her schedule allowed. Her health did not permit her to come to England again. An eagerly awaited reunion with Isabel never occurred. There's an anguished note in Frances's journal for New Year's Eve, 1896: "Why must Isabel & I be separated? Because we put our Work before our Love ..."

Whilst the exact nature of the relationship between Isabel and Frances remains a matter of speculation, there was undoubtedly a close bond between them – a bond not just of affection but of shared faith and a desire to work for the benefit of all humanity. Through these two women the 'special relationship' between Britain and America was strengthened in the cause of temperance.

Following Frances' death, Isabel succeeded her as President of the WWCTU. "Hereditary succession," sniped Josephine Butler. Isabel continued to lead the NBWTA until 1903, when ill-health forced her to retire from the role. Two other factors probably also influenced this decision – a frustration with temperance politics and a desire to do more hands-on work. The association presented her with a flattering address and a cheque towards another of her projects – a settlement in Bow.

This scheme, in the East End of London, operated between 1900 and 1905. Isabel was helped by Evelyn Bateman who had managed the Ledbury mission so successfully. Life was hard and Isabel would work indefatigably to help the poor families there, ready to go out at all times of the day or night to avert crises. Isabel had a room within the settlement, amongst the "incessant traffic, unsavoury smells and ceaseless activity".

There were clubs for men, women and children, with regular Band of Hope meetings to encourage all the children to respect and keep their temperance pledge. Isabel also opened a restaurant next to the meeting hall to provide cheap, nourishing food for the factory girls. There was also a small hospital. With alcohol dependence a big issue, Isabel pioneered an out-patients service in The Strand, where those who could not manage a months' stay in hospital could attend three times a day for treatment under the Oppenheimer regime. "Most marvellous results were obtained," recorded Miss Bateman in notes found in the Eastnor Castle archives.

Whilst working in the East End, Isabel had a house built for herself in Woodford, but the original size and design was scaled back significantly, presumably to cut costs. She would travel from Bow to Woodford on the tube, often in the nurse's uniform which she favoured – a real woman of the people. However she never made the Woodford house her permanent home.

Isabel was starting to appreciate that society had changed significantly since she had first started 'preaching temperance' in the late 1880s. She felt that, now, there was a better understanding of the "whole pathology of drunkenness". She even went so far as to say, in a speech to the NBWTA in 1904, "… such words as those of the great surgeon, Sir Frederick Treves, are likely to produce a far greater arrest of thought, and in the end, wider results, than all the temperance meetings that have ever been held."

Although she remained president of the WWCTU until 1906, Isabel became increasingly focused on life at Duxhurst. She lived simply, either at The Cottage or in her London flat in Gray's Inn. She remained hugely popular and influential. In 1907 she was voted the woman readers of the London Evening News would most like to have as the first female prime minister.

Isabel, the aristocrat, had fought and won those inner battles with her conscience. In her later years, she seems to have distanced herself, physically and emotionally, from her upbringing.

The terms of her father's will allowed her to sign over the Reigate estates to her son on his marriage. Reigate Priory Park was sold in 1920. Bought by a local merchant, Randal Vogan, it was then generously donated to the town. All the Somers' other Reigate estates were also sold. Although this occurred shortly after Isabel's death, her son had previously consulted her about his plans and she had been in full agreement. Most of the houses and businesses in Reigate were offered to existing tenants on advantageous terms, with mortgages also arranged. This became known as 'The Great Sale of Reigate' – a sign of changing times and another nail in the coffin of the strict class structure into which Isabel had been born. The Priory itself was sold separately and all manorial rights were relinquished to the council.

By 1913, she allowed her cousin Arthur, the heir to the Somers' estates, to take the reins at Eastnor. She still liked to visit and she still used the properties as locations for fundraising and philanthropic activities. Isabel's friend and colleague, Mary Ward Poole, wrote a wonderful description of visits to Eastnor. Initially she noted how children would curtsey when Isabel appeared in the village but soon they realized that she didn't wish them to stand on ceremony. So instead the children would "go up to her smiling and unafraid; school children, choir boys and village girls would be seen during preparations for Christmas plays lolling in happy abandonment on gorgeous crimson brocaded chairs in the Great Hall waiting for rehearsals, careless of the eye of the old housekeeper who would be in and out looking unspeakable things at such liberties taken".

When war came, the Red Cross requisitioned the manor house at Duxhurst and many of the women patients were dispersed throughout the country. Some, however, stayed on to nurse the soldiers or to care for the children who remained in the village. More children arrived, for Isabel's new cause was the welfare of the innocent illegitimate babies whose numbers understandably increased during the war. By 1917, there were over 500 applications for places at Duxhurst, some from the mothers themselves, others from hospitals and institutions.

Isabel became such an acknowledged expert in the field of childcare that she was invited to give evidence at the 1920 Hopkinson Committee on Adoption. She was in favour of keeping mothers and children together wherever possible, although she had also witnessed at first hand many situations where this was not in the best interests of the child. For her, the child's welfare should always come first.

Isabel died in 1921, aged 69. She had made it known that burial in the family vaults of Eastnor Castle was not for her. She had asked for a simple service at her London Church, St Albans in Holborn (near her flat in Gray's Inn), led by her cousin the Rev E F Russell. But that simple service was attended by representatives from the NBWTA, the Salvation Army and a myriad of organizations with which Isabel had been associated. Wreaths were sent by Queen Mary and Queen Alexandra.

Glowing obituaries comparing her to Florence Nightingale

appeared in the press. Isabel had never thought she deserved praise for her work. But on two levels she had made a huge difference. She had spearheaded the women's campaign for temperance, not just in Britain but across the world. And she had touched the lives of many individuals by her compassion and small gestures of kindness.

CHAPTER 10

Rosalind Howard, Countess of Carlisle (1845 – 1921) – 'The Radical Countess'

"A very independent member of a very independent family," wrote the MP, TP O'Connor in an obituary of Rosalind Howard in *The Telegraph* in August 1921.

More recently she has been described as "one of the most problematic women to espouse the temperance cause" and an "awkward choice" to succeed Lady Henry Somerset. (Margaret Barrow in *Alcohol and Temperance in Modern History: A Global Encyclopaedia* by Jack S Blocker Jr, David M Fahey and Ian R Tyrell 2003)

Rosalind followed Lady Henry (Isabel) Somerset as President of both the National British Women's Temperance Association (NBWTA) and The World Woman's Christian Temperance Union (WWCTU). Although they shared an aristocratic background, the two women could hardly have been more different. Whilst Isabel was renowned for her kindness, tolerance and pragmatism, Rosalind Howard – at least in mid and later life – was an autocrat, with a fiery temper and a dominating character. She had little respect for those who dared to hold opinions different from her own. Yet she did some important work on the temperance stage and helped raise the cause up the political agenda.

Born in 1845, Rosalind came from a somewhat eccentric family who seemed to delight in heated argument and debate. Her father, Lord Stanley of Alderley, was lampooned as Sir Benjamin Backbite, so notorious was he for outspoken comments about others, especially his fellow politicians. Her mother was responsible for Rosalind's education, a liberal one for the time. A dutiful wife during her husband's lifetime, Lady Stanley was also a strong-willed woman who, in 1869, became one of the founders of Girton College, Cambridge. Kate, one of Rosalind's sisters, was a fierce feminist; she supported equal pay, equality of education and birth control. Sadly she died aged just 30, leaving a young family including a son Bertrand Russell who became a great philosopher. Rosalind's eldest brother, Henry, caused a stir by marrying his African mistress and converting to the Muslim faith. Rosalind, perhaps, had needed to develop strong views and opinions of her own in order to have a voice within such a family.

Like all daughters of the aristocracy, however well educated they were, Rosalind was expected to make a good marriage. She caught the eye of several young men, including the poet, Wilfred Scawen Blunt, a self-confessed rake. However, it was George Howard whose suit was accepted. Rosalind was still in her teens and George proposed as soon as he had graduated from Cambridge. The young couple married in 1864. George was a keen and gifted artist who would eventually succeed his uncle to the Earldom of Carlisle. It seemed a true love match but Rosalind perhaps recognised immediately that George was a malleable man, someone who would allow her to express her strong personality. She wanted to use her "influence to make him [George] all I think he is capable of becoming, good, happy and useful himself ... and not waste his life".

George was not particularly interested in politics, despite his father being an MP. In fact, when his father was campaigning, it was Rosalind, not George, who helped him. After his father's death, George did stand as MP for East Cumberland and Rosalind again proved herself an adept campaigner, canvassing on his behalf, although not speaking from the platform.

The couple enjoyed a close, passionate relationship for many years. Theirs did not seem to be the typical straight-laced Victorian marriage. George would make intimate drawings of his wife and often sent these as tokens of his love when he was away from her. But Rosalind was always the feistier of the two and George would usually concede to her wishes. They had 11 children (one of whom died in infancy) and led what, to the outside world, would have seemed a charmed life. They travelled extensively, George particularly enjoying the light and architecture of Italy. They were on close terms with the artistic glitterati of the day – William Morris, George Frederick Watts, Rossetti and Burne-Jones amongst them. Their London home, at Palace Green, was designed for them by their friend Philip Webb.

George became increasingly occupied with his own painting and his patronage of the arts, including his role as Trustee of the National Gallery. Rosalind meanwhile became increasingly focused on the Cumberland estates at Naworth (near Brampton) and Castle Howard in Yorkshire. She loved the rugged countryside and she didn't just take a passing interest in estate matters; she immersed herself fully, effectively acting as her husband's land agent. She would go to livestock sales and know exactly the value of every bull. She studied the accounts and took the responsibilities of landowner very seriously.

She also took an interest in local politics and became increasingly frustrated that George paid so little attention to these matters. Her acerbic personality started to manifest itself more strongly. Within their family circle, she was already being accused of "uninhibited tactlessness".

Rosalind was a woman in need of a conviction or purpose. It seemed that marriage and motherhood weren't sufficient to occupy her intellect and organizational skills. Indeed, when young, her children saw little of her; she never put them to bed or read stories to them, although she did lead them on occasional expeditions and picnics.

Then, in 1881, when a visiting mission arrived in the small hamlet of Lanercost, near Naworth, Rosalind was won over to the temperance cause. She embraced it with a fierce passion and, as she described it, with "the enthusiasm of those who rejoice to have found a new and better way".

She had become very aware of the problems caused by the heavy drinking amongst the locals. She took the pledge and made all her children do so as well. Before long she had even persuaded George to abstain.

On New Year's Day 1882, Rosalind held a large gathering at Tweed Mill, near Brampton. She invited not just the local tradesmen but all the poor of the area. She laid on a fine party, with presents, prizes and a special tea. It was the launch of her personal temperance campaign. Many took the pledge, whether out of genuine belief that it was the right thing to do or because they feared the indomitable lady we can't say. What we do know is that the police recorded that they had never experienced such a sober festive period in Cumberland.

After that party, Rosalind wrote to her mother. "We are only on the threshold, we have not won our victory yet … Till the public houses shut up entirely we have won no permanent or decisive success."

She started to hold weekly meetings, recognizing that people needed on-going support to remain constant to their pledge. Surprisingly, as her son-in-law noted in his 1962 biography of Rosalind, there were no female speakers at these meetings and no women on the local committees.

By the end of her first 12 months of campaigning for temperance, over 1,500 people had signed the pledge. Later, Rosalind would comment, no doubt with great frustration, "If it had been possible at that time to get a local veto poll, without doubt Brampton would have been cleared of public houses and become a prohibition area." She believed local opinion was firmly against the drinking of alcohol.

In due course Rosalind would make taking the pledge a condition of tenancy on the estates. She closed eight public houses, and then leased one to be used as a 'free and easy coffee house' for the working men. It no doubt helped that her husband, George, was the chairman of the local licensing board. The pub in the archway over the entrance to the drive at Castle Howard was closed. Rosalind had half the building converted into a guest house or rest home for women to come for a month's convalescence. These were women who had been recommended, not because they were desperately poor, but because they needed practical, physical and moral help. Referrals were made by other women "of sense and experience" not, as would normally have been the case for such charitable enterprises, by clergy. Rosalind clearly felt women understood the trials and tribulations of females better than men did.

She bought one pub in Cumberland, The Plough Inn, with the specific intent of getting its licence withdrawn. The local brewers ceremoniously buried the signboard, apparently reciting over it, "Ashes to ashes, dust to dust, If the Countess won't have you, the Devil must."

As early as 1883, the drink trade in the area had suffered a major collapse. "The publicans are really angry now," wrote Rosalind. A further mission resulted in another 300 people taking the pledge. Rosalind noted with satisfaction, "the reverent, thoughtful look of the low class which came night after night, listening to speeches and hymns."

The Castle Howard estate became the venue for annual temperance demonstrations and galas. There was free admission to the park, but a charge of six pence to view the Castle and Pleasure Gardens and 12 hours of continuous entertainment, including performances from local temperance bands and choirs, cricket matches and displays of the garden fountains. Temperance was becoming a by-word for fun and Rosalind Howard should be given some credit for this.

Despite her high profile temperance work, Rosalind didn't give up serving wine to her family or guests until after she was elected as president of the NBWTA in 1903. After that, visitors had to accept the no alcohol rule.

Her belief in the need to educate children about the perils of drink was something she would continue to practise for the rest of her life. Sadly, she became so fixated with the matter that she could not forgive two of her sons when they took up drinking again as young men. But at this stage she was focused, to good effect, on expanding the local Band of Hope groups. By the end of 1882 there were 331 children enrolled.

Rosalind also initiated holidays for children from the industrial towns of Leeds, Bradford and Huddersfield, placing them with estate workers in cottages on the estate. She devised an effective way of securing places. Her own offspring were made to write many letters asking for both money and accommodation for the children. Each recipient of such a letter was asked to write in similar vein to six others. 'Snowball' letters, her daughter Dorothy called them.

Rosalind's brand of philanthropy was not to encourage dependency on hand-outs. She condemned the "methods of pauperising" of some of her fellow social reformers. But she didn't usually carry out her social work in person. The actual "slumming" was left to her children or trusty colleagues.

Despite her new enthusiasm for temperance and social reform, Rosalind still accompanied her husband on many of his painting trips abroad. She may have tolerated, rather than encouraged, his art, but she perhaps also appreciated that his preoccupation gave her greater scope for influence.

By 1886, Rosalind was managing all the family estates, some

78,000 acres, and her husband was very happy to let her do so. This arrangement was very unusual for its time and no doubt raised a few eyebrows in aristocratic circles. But this wouldn't have bothered either Rosalind or George. Rosalind's shrewd management was effective; she managed to clear the estates of large debts which had been accumulated during the gambling years of a previous Earl.

Rosalind engrossed herself in politics. Her nickname, "The Radical Countess", was well-deserved. She promoted Liberal ideals, temperance, women's suffrage and, critically, Home Rule for Ireland (the devolution of many powers from the British parliament to the Irish themselves). Rosalind's family had strong Irish connections, so her interest in the subject was perhaps not surprising. In 1914, she very publically made a £300 donation to the Irish National Volunteer Movement. However, George was firmly opposed to Home Rule. He had known one of the victims of the 'activists'. Rosalind saw George's position as a personal betrayal. He was no longer the malleable husband of their youth.

"Politics are rapidly becoming a totally tabooed subject here which does not make life easier," Rosalind complained to her mother. But her mother was unsympathetic, showing a clear understanding of the intractability of her daughter. "You seem to be in a state in which you should be taken away from your family and placed on a high mountain." Perhaps Lady Stanley could see that Rosalind's intransigence was destroying the marriage.

Rosalind's obituary in *The Times* on August 13th, 1921 makes clear the popular view of Rosalind's behaviour at this time: "… London Society was intolerant of Home Rulers, and still more so of a woman who preached Home Rule against her husband's wishes. A worldly woman would have tried to make her peace with society. A very tactful and conciliatory one might have succeeded. But Mrs Howard was utterly unworldly, cared little for tact, and despised conciliation."

When the two parliamentary seats of East Cumberland were reduced to one, George decided not to stand again for election. His wife, it is safe to assume, would have gladly taken his place. It would be too simple to say that politics drove Rosalind and George apart. The different personalities of the two, which in the earlier part of their marriage had been complementary, became irreconcilable. George had at this stage turned elsewhere (to Maisie, his wife's sister-in-law) for the love and affection he no longer found with Rosalind.

Sadly, as the marriage disintegrated, the children were forced to take sides – the sons primarily with their father, the daughters with their mother. Many tales of Rosalind's extreme rudeness and temper have been told. Virginia Surtees' book *The Artist and The Autocrat* published in 1988 perpetuates some of these stories. It is often difficult to separate myth from fact. But her daughter Dorothy gives a candid appraisal. "Tempests were touched off by questions of sex, or of jealousy for power, or of Radicalism which she held with burning zeal." Yet Dorothy also admired her mother in many ways, describing her as an hypnotic speaker, "compelling and uninterruptable".

Despite the occasional estrangement, both before and after her marriage to Francis Henley, Dorothy worked alongside her mother in temperance campaigns, as did her sister Cecelia. Ironically, Francis was a brewer so this must have been a difficult match for Rosalind to accept. She greeted news of the engagement with "the insanity of rage uncontrolled" and didn't attend the wedding. Yet ultimately Rosalind affected a reconciliation, although with no apology.

One of Rosalind's sons-in-law, Charles Roberts, in his biography *The Radical Countess*, acknowledges that her "devastating anger left incurable wounds". Her "vehement temper", reined in during the first half of her life, now often seemed out of control.

Daughter Mary was once so bold as to call her mother an "egotist". As she explained, "You [Rosalind] must do what you want to do for other people. It's your will, not theirs, that must be done."

Tragically, three of the Howard sons died young; Christopher whom Rosalind never forgave for becoming a heavy drinker, Herbert who died in battle but whose gambling debts ensured he had lost all favour with his mother, and Oliver, with whom Rosalind had always had a difficult relationship. When another son, Charley, married against her wishes, Rosalind was so furious that she forbade her daughters to be bridesmaids and refused to attend the ceremony herself. She was outraged that Charley had had the audacity to choose a Tory as his bride. Yet she allowed the newlyweds to use Naworth for their honeymoon, personally supervising the preparations for their stay.

Politics drove a wedge not just between Rosalind and her husband but also between her and many of their circle. Rosalind became increasingly bitter and even old friends commented that she was "hard". She wrote of "enduring" life rather than enjoying it. Was this was just her personality, or did she have undiagnosed mental health problems? Sir William Broadbent, physician to Queen Victoria and a renowned neurologist, told Rosalind that she had "nervous bankruptcy", perhaps a kinder phrase than 'nervous breakdown'.

On occasions, Rosalind did show considerable self-awareness. She knew she could upset people with her brusque manner. In June 1906, she wrote a letter to Agnes Slack, secretary of the NBWTA, actually apologising for upsetting her. She talked of how strain and excitement "often make me impatient and hurried in manner and as I am by nature impetuous and impulsive I know that the excited mental strain on top of that nature must constantly make me a horrid fellow-worker". She acknowledged that she had changed since the "sunny days" of her youth "when my health was so strong and my spirits so radian and I was not … troubled, over-hurried, over-sensitive, impatient …"

Not surprisingly, with her heavy workload, Rosalind's physical health suffered, although some, including her daughters, suggest that her heart problems were imaginary or exaggerated. It was, and still is, common to blame physical, rather than mental, ailments for one's inaction. It is seen as more socially acceptable. But Rosalind's use of dramatic language, such as "it would be too dangerous for me to attend", when excusing herself from meetings, gives clues as to her inner agitation. For the last 20 years of her life, Rosalind felt "spent" yet she continued to push all her causes. In that letter to Agnes Slack she wrote of being "relentlessly pressed by such accumulated tasks that I can never overtake my duties or my opportunities". This is a telling observation. She was clearly frustrated that she lacked the energy not only to do what she had to do but also what she wanted to do. She had a position of wealth and influence and she clearly didn't feel she was making the best use of it. Her many achievements should be seen in this context.

Rosalind would employ secretaries and paid organisers, constantly writing letters, policies and procedures. She became obsessed with the need for lists, even down to detailed inventories of bed linen – another indication of a troubled mind? She commandeered her daughters, especially Dorothy and Cecelia, to deputise for her at many meetings, although where possible she remained an "assiduous committee woman", pushing herself to attend meetings and make long journeys to London. On temperance matters, a subject on which their views coincided, her husband would often speak on her behalf if she was indisposed. He even accompanied their daughter, Dorothy, to the 1906 WWCTU conference in Boston as Rosalind's representative.

Rosalind turned increasingly to a young man, Leif Jones, who had originally joined the household as a tutor. Leif Jones shared

Rosalind's views on politics and temperance. He had the unenviable task of trying to work for both Rosalind and George, becoming both a buffer and a conduit for necessary communication between the warring couple.

Inevitably, Leif Jones became known as 'Tea Leaf Jones' as he took on wider public duties. In 1905 he became an MP. Whenever Rosalind was in London, she would wait up eager to hear all the news of the day's debates in parliament from Leif Jones or from the MPs in her family – her son, Geoffrey or son-in-law Charles Roberts. She could have sat in the Ladies' Gallery (behind the iron grill so detested by the suffragettes) or in the Peeresses' Gallery but in fact she rarely visited the Palace of Westminster herself. Perhaps that would have been just too frustrating for her. In 1932, Leif Jones was elevated to the peerage as Lord Rhayder. When Sir Wifred Lawson, MP and leader of the United Kingdom Alliance (UKA), died, it was Leif Jones who took over as Alliance President.

Rosalind knew Sir Wilfred well. His land abutted the Howard's Cumberland estates. The UKA had been working relentlessly for prohibition. As a first step towards this, the Alliance supported the Direct Veto so locals could block the issue or renewal of licences in their area. However, the UKA, and Rosalind, didn't agree that those who had lost their licences should be paid compensation. As a member of the NBWTA, Rosalind clashed with its then president, Isabel Somerset, over this policy. Isabel, unlike Rosalind, thought any small step in reducing licences was worth having. When Rosalind became President of the NBWTA, in one month alone, she sent out over 4,000 letters and leaflets, attacking the compensation policy. She felt it artificially raised the value of licensed premises. Moreover, the compensation levy, ostensibly paid by the drink trade, was effectively public money because licence duties were taxpayers' money.

Rosalind was not afraid of the 'P word', as she referred to

'prohibition'. She didn't want pubs to become "more wholesome", she wanted them shunned and preferably banned altogether. Under her presidency, the NBWTA raised money for the UKA – almost £800 from one event alone. Rosalind said this "demonstrated to the country that the NBWTA stands unreservedly for Prohibition".

Sir Wilfred Lawson was also a staunch Liberal. Rosalind joined the Women's Liberal Federation (WLF) in 1890. She had been encouraged to do so by no less a figure than Mrs Gladstone, wife of the Prime Minister. Initially Rosalind had refused to join the WLF because it was not actively supporting the campaign for women's suffrage. In typical style, Rosalind set out to change this stance. She became president of the WLF in 1902, a position she held until her death in 1921. She led the 'Progressives' within the NLF, yet some within the party thought she was not sufficiently committed to the cause. For each year there was a vote as to whether the Federation should refuse to back any Liberal parliamentary candidate who did not actively support women's suffrage; each year Rosalind and, by varying margins, the Federation, voted against such a stance. In 1891, she felt the Irish Home Rule policy should take precedence over votes for women. In 1914, Rosalind was still refusing to accept the issue of support for women's suffrage as a 'test question', claiming that no one reform should be pushed in this isolated manner and possibly endanger all the rest of the Liberal's legislative programme of social reform.

Rosalind firmly believed in the inevitability of women's suffrage. In her lifetime she had already witnessed great strides in women's education and seen Scotland grant limited voting rights in municipal elections to women. As early as 1883, a parliamentary motion for women's suffrage had been defeated by just 130 votes to 114, though subsequent bills failed by larger majorities. Rosalind had seen the first women doctors and also the first strikes by female workers. She'd witnessed and supported the Local Government Act of 1894 which abolished the five property qualifications for Poor Law Guardians, making many more women eligible to stand for election for these positions, something they did to very good effect. She firmly believed that women wanted to be taken seriously, that they didn't want to be condemned to a life of frivolity, rather to be weaned from it.

She belonged to the National Union of Women's Suffrage Societies (NUWSS) founded in 1897, with its motto "Faith, perseverance, patience". She was certainly well regarded by its leader, Millicent Fawcett, who declared that Lady Carlisle's campaigning was "worth at least 20 votes in the division".

But Rosalind was not a suffragette. She took great care to distance herself and the NBWTA from meetings, marches or demonstrations where suffragettes would also be present. She abhorred the violent antics of the Pankhursts and their fellow protesters. "It is we, the law abiding, patient, constitutional all-round reforming women, who are winning the day," she wrote, "and the impatient, lawless, scolding women with hate in their hearts are only setting our cause back." High profile suffragette protests at the House of Commons she declared "appallingly shocking". With Rosalind's fiery temperament, the country could perhaps be thankful that she was on the side of peaceful protest.

However, Rosalind was very open in linking her temperance work with her support for women's suffrage. Not only would she urge NBWTA members to support Liberal candidates who wanted to extend the vote to more women, she encouraged fellow Liberals to embrace the temperance cause. In 1904, she persuaded the NBWTA's Executive to pass a resolution that a "special whip be sent to all members of Parliament urging them to be in their places on March 16th to vote for Sir Charles McLaren's resolution re the extension of the Franchise to women".

She would certainly have agreed with the words of Alice Smith in an article which appeared in the NBWTA journal, *The White*

Ribbon in 1907. "To be included amongst the various classes of irresponsibles – the lunatic, the pauper and criminal, is an insult to womanhood and a disgrace to English manhood."

Rosalind did exercise her legal right as a woman aged over 30 to stand for the local councils and in 1894 she was elected onto both the Brampton Parish and the District Councils. She held these offices for several years. The council meetings became popular with the public and it wasn't just an interest in local affairs which drew people in. It was the frequent heated exchanges between Rosalind and her Tory adversary and local publican, Mr Winthrop. Rosalind's daughter Dorothy frequently attended these 'Fortnightly Entertainments', as they became known. She recalls how Mr Winthrop was "regularly primed to be just drunk enough to bait my mother for the joy of the onlookers who crowded in".

By 1913, perhaps to appeal to some of the doubters within the NBWTA, the call for women's suffrage was being linked by Rosalind and others to religion; "electoral power, if wielded in a God-fearing way, is a mighty weapon for the redemption of the people from the intemperance, vice and abject poverty, which drag down and destroy life of so large a part of the community." This had strong echoes of Frances Willard's 'Home Protection' policy, so heavily endorsed by Isabel Somerset. Yet Rosalind, some argue, was at this stage of her life, an atheist or free thinker. Even her daughter Dorothy thought it strange that Rosalind worked so closely with evangelical temperance reformers, given her own lack of faith. Perhaps, in this regard at least, Rosalind was showing some element of pragmatism.

Rosalind had the distinction of being the first woman to serve as the President of a mixed gender temperance organization when in 1892 she took that office in the North of England Temperance League. This, however, was primarily an honorary role. A title always helped.

When Lady Henry Somerset retired as president of the NBWTA

in 1903, citing health reasons, Rosalind was duly elected, although not unanimously. She had never been in favour of the 'Americanisation' of the Association or the 'Do Everything Policy' so beloved by her predecessor and by Frances Willard. She soon closed down many of the departments within the NBWTA which were dealing with what she deemed to be non-essential matters. However, the need for an electoral policy was deemed paramount. So she established a 'political and women's suffrage department', headed by one of her staunch supporters, Miss Bertha Mason.

Kathleen Fitzpatrick comments that after Isabel Somerset's retirement the NBWTA "settled down to the quiet respectability from which she [Isabel Somerset] had raised it." This is an observation blinkered by loyalty to a friend. For, under Rosalind Howard, the NBWTA remained respectable but it certainly wasn't quiet. It became increasingly political and pro-prohibition. Rosalind was strong in her condemnation of the drink trade, calling it "England's most dangerous foe … which lives and thrives on sorrow and degradation of our people".

There is a strange omission from the Annual Reports of the NBWTA under Rosalind's presidency. There is no 'President's Address' prior to all the other reports being presented. It seems Rosalind chose not to prepare a speech or to commit to addressing the audience at any specific time. Instead she would deliver a stirring oration when she felt it appropriate, always full of detail and cogent argument. Jennie Street, an NBWTA member wrote in *Christian Word* that Rosalind had "a rather Quakerly inclination to wait for the moving of the Spirit". This must have been a nightmare for the secretary, dutifully trying to record events and for the press who chose to feature the NBWTA annual conventions. They had the task of trying to summarise her "impressive and inspiring" addresses. But Rosalind's words were perhaps more powerful because they were from the heart and of the moment.

Rosalind's daughter, Cecelia, also served on the NBWTA's national executive council. She too was an inspiring speaker but she presented a softer side to the Howard's reforming zeal.

Rosalind continued to promote women's work at a local level, encouraging NBWTA branches in their support for their local temperance halls. In some areas, the women helped set up coffee houses and refreshment stalls at fairs. Factory girls were invited to attend special temperance meetings during their tea and dinner breaks. In 1907, Rosalind launched a special pledge-taking campaign, funding most of the work herself. Another 2,500 names were collected. Carefully preserved in the Castle Howard archives is one of Rosalind's own pledge books.

The Association campaigned for special children's courts and supported the work of the Police Court Missionaries. These missionaries were initially the idea of the Church of England Temperance Society but many local branches of the NBWTA adopted this work. Effectively the Police Court Missionaries were early probation officers and many were women, working with "our tempted sisters". With the consent of the magistrate, a Police Court Missionary could take charge of young women brought before the bench on drink related offences. Having met with the prisoners in their cells or the waiting room before they were called into court, they would remain throughout the hearing and often be able to intercede to arrange for payment of fines. The missionary would find the offender a new home or position and work with them to improve their self-respect and desist from alcohol.

A promotional booklet by the South Metropolitan Union of branches of the NBWTA produced in 1904 declared, "It is obvious that when women and girls are the offenders, a woman's insight, loving sympathy, and tactful advice are indispensible." Soon many cases under the First Offenders Act were passed over to NBWTA missionaries. Special homes were set up, including a House of Help in Greenwich which could accommodate 20 women at a time and help over 5,000 women in any one year.

Another area of work which Rosalind thought particularly important was scientific temperance instruction (STI). She urged that schools should teach children about the dangers of alcohol. She also recognized that the arguments against alcohol had to be founded on solid research not just emotion. The NBWTA and the TAU drafted an STI curriculum based on the work of an American woman, Mary Hunt. But STI was to be a short-lived experiment in Britain, although it had more success in some American states.

The NBWTA had also joined with other temperance organizations to establish the Temperance Collegiate Association, to educate people, especially those who wished to work in the temperance cause, about both the physical and social effects of alcohol consumption. Under Rosalind's presidency, this support continued and women took prominent roles on the Collegiate Association's executive committee.

Rosalind was approached to take over the presidency of the World Woman's Christian Temperance Union (WWCTU) when Isabel Somerset resigned in 1906. Although she had been a member of the Union for some time, Rosalind was initially quite dismissive of its influence. "In England no-one cares a bit about the world movement," she said. Nor was she impressed with the way it operated. She felt there was not sufficient control over the way its five main officers ran affairs, with only a convention every two years to consider policies and priorities. In her opinion, there were more differences than similarities between America and Britain.

This was one of several issues over which she clashed with Agnes Slack, secretary of the NBWTA and editor of its journal during Rosalind's presidency. Agnes was a highly influential temperance reformer, Liberal and suffrage campaigner in her own right. She went on to become president of the NBWTA in 1925, after Rosalind's death and after the subsequent three year tenure of Rosalind's daughter, Lady Cecilia Roberts. She also took on the role of British Secretary for the WWCTU.

Of necessity, Agnes and Rosalind had a close working relationship, one which survived, even perhaps thrived, because the pair would be frank with each other. Agnes learnt to answer back and hold her own ground. She was frequently invited by Rosalind to stay at Naworth or Castle Howard so they could plan and prepare for meetings. Like the majority of the women committee members of both the NBWTA and the WWCTU, Agnes enjoyed the grandeur of the Howard estates and walking in the footsteps of such luminaries as Harriet Beecher Stowe, Alfred Tennyson and Burne Jones. She would write up reports of such gatherings, referring to Rosalind's hospitality in glowing terms. Occasionally this 'obsequiousness' would grate with Rosalind. In 1910, she ordered Agnes to "strike out the paragraph about my entertaining the NEC [National Executive Committee] at Castle Howard. I do not approve of personal puffs. We can use those four lines for something more important". It's possible that, in some ways, Rosalind was also jealous of Agnes – she was younger, more energetic and unencumbered by family and landowner responsibilities.

Rosalind could well afford to be generous with her hospitality. It also made sense, to her at least, that if she felt unable to attend national executive council meetings in London, or world conventions abroad, the women delegates could come to her. She enjoyed hearing all the news of international campaigns, though sometimes she felt too fatigued to make the most of the opportunity to meet foreign delegates, something she found very frustrating. She would also accommodate 'Y' groups – young women aged 14 to 18 – at the Castle Howard Guest House, charging her daughters Dorothy and Aurea to look after them.

Rosalind's husband, George, and her protégé Leif Jones, spoke regularly at NBWTA annual council meetings. For Rosalind recognised that women couldn't achieve temperance legislation by themselves; with no vote, they needed men to see it through. But the women could do "the patient, out-of-sight service, educating, preparing the public mind, winning individuals".

Once elected as president of the world union, Rosalind made some key changes. The five officers of the WWCTU effectively became a standing committee, allowing more to be done between conventions. Rosalind herself didn't travel to WWCTU meetings, claiming ill-health, but her correspondence on its behalf and with the Union's officers was substantial. She sometimes sent her daughters Dorothy or Cecelia in her place. Dorothy called the WWCTU conference in Boston "an orgy of Hot-Gospelling", something Rosalind might have found hard to accept. Gradually, though, she started to see the potential of a world-wide organization. She also made significant financial contributions to the WWCTU's work, including £1,000 in 1910. Much of this went to fund overseas temperance missionaries.

In subsequent years, the WWCTU stubbornly refused to allow Rosalind to resign, even when she had made it patently clear that she didn't wish to continue her involvement. Her failing health, excessive fatigue and countless other duties meant Rosalind felt she couldn't devote enough time or energy to the world cause. In the Union's elections for president in 1913, as reported in *The New York Times*, Rosalind received 308 votes out of a possible 379. All the English delegates (who perhaps understood that Rosalind meant what she said) had voted for another candidate, Mrs Stevens; all the rest insisted on voting for Rosalind Carlisle.

Mrs Stevens said she would only agree to be Vice-President to Rosalind's Presidency. She admitted to having written to Rosalind about the matter, with assurances that the WWCTU didn't wish her to work so hard. She had received no reply. Perhaps it was the comment that "we do wish to have her name as our chief officer for the influence it will have not only in America but all over Europe" which annoyed Rosalind. The temperance women still seemed to be in search of their 'titled figurehead', not a role either Isabel Somerset or Rosalind Carlisle had ever wished to embrace. Effectively despite her express wishes, Rosalind did continue as WWCTU president until her death and her daughter Lady Aurea Howard remained actively involved long after.

An unexpected consequence of Rosalind's work was the spread of the women's temperance movement to Germany. Ottilie Hoffman had been governess to Rosalind's children. She had embraced the message that abstinence was the only solution to the drink problem. When she returned to Germany, she set up an organization there, Frauenbund fur alcoholfreie Kulture. This became known as the German Union. Ottilie went on to receive honours for her social work. In 1909, by official military order, five hundred copies of her paper *Abstinez* were distributed to soldiers. Sixteen officers, in full uniform, were ordered to attend a meeting of the women's German Union. In the BWTA's centenary booklet, *A Century of Service*, the comment is well made, "It may be said that Fraulein Hoffman was the Mother of the German Union; it might also be said that Lady Carlisle was its grandmother".

One wonders whether Rosalind was over-conscious of following in Isabel Somerset's footsteps, despite being slightly older. Although in many ways fighting the same battles, the two women had clashed on several occasions. Rosalind even complained that Isabel had tried to undermine her candidacy for president, although there is no evidence to this effect. But whilst Isabel was now actively campaigning for the Gothenburg system of disinterested or public management, Rosalind was adamantly opposed to it and the NBWTA backed her in this. She accused Isabel of sowing dissension within temperance ranks. Correspondence between the two women became quite frosty.

This difficult relationship continued even to the time of Isabel's resignation as president of the WWCTU, with Rosalind refusing to sanction a NBWTA donation to a testimonial fund for the departing president. However, the animosity was softened when Isabel offered congratulations and assistance to Rosalind when she was elected. In 1906, Rosalind was credited with persuading Isabel, as an ex-president, to attend to WWCTU Convention in America. In 1914 Isabel was invited, at Rosalind's special request, to attend the NBWTA's national executive committee meeting to talk about the work of the WWCTU.

Although at times Rosalind seemed to divide opinion, she actually tried to effect a reconciliation between the two factions of the old BWTA. As detailed in the previous chapter, in 1893, under Isabel Somerset's presidency, there had been a big split in the ranks. Those who wanted the Association to concentrate all its efforts on temperance reform had broken away and formed the Total Abstinence Union (TAU). In 1906, it was Rosalind who urged both groups "to stand shoulder to shoulder" and co-operate with the UKA to organize large demonstrations in favour of Local Veto. However, she failed to achieve a merger between the two groups; it took until 1926 for this to happen.

In 1904 A Liquor Licensing Act was passed by the Conservative government which gave compensation to those who had lost their alcohol licence. The NBWTA, with Rosalind at the helm, was not happy. It supported the Liberal Party's proposals for much more limited compensation.

When the Liberal party came into office, their licensing bill of 1908, which embodied many temperance reforms, was passed by the House of Commons but defeated in the Lords. According to *The Daily News* on 28th November 1908, the defeat was down to "the startled terror of financiers and shareholders". As we shall see in the conclusion, this was the truth but not the whole truth.

Rosalind took the defeat hard but persisted with her campaigns. In 1908, she and the Women's Liberal Association urged Parliament to pass legislation to prohibit the employment of women (except wives, widows and daughters of publicans) in licensed premises. Signatories to the petition included Lady Elizabeth Biddulph of the TAU and Florence Bramwell-Booth of the Salvation Army. However, not all women agreed. A Barmaids' Defence League was established to fight the measure, as some wanted to keep all opportunities for employment open to all women.

To those who shared her views, Rosalind was generous with her time and praise, recognizing their contributions to the cause. "She was good when charging at the head of her troops," wrote her son-in-law and fellow Liberal, Gilbert Murray, "but I suppose if she was not quite the head she left the troops altogether." Yet, behind the scenes, she was also seen as a "guide, philosopher and friend to many temperance leaders of both sexes", according to an obituary in *The White Ribbon Memorial Number* in 1921. As with any description of Rosalind, there's a sting in the tail even of this tribute. It continued, "And woe to anyone either in private or public who ventured a passage with her on matters with which they were imperfectly acquainted."

Rosalind's husband, George, died in 1911. Marriage hadn't stopped Rosalind campaigning for the causes she believed in, and widowhood hardly dented her public persona.

Then came war and other battles became more pressing than the temperance one. Rosalind was a fierce supporter of the war yet she adamantly refused to have a regiment stationed at Castle Howard and was appalled at the idea of the house being requisitioned by the army. She took in refugees from Belgium, although she did expect them to work and she insisted they be teetotal. They renovated some of the pitmen's cottages on the estate which had fallen into an appalling condition.

According to *The Times,* Rosalind's behaviour was becoming increasingly erratic, her judgments sometime "unreal". She certainly provided good copy for the newspapers. "1,000 bottles of wine wasted" screamed the headlines when the story broke about a huge amount of claret being poured away at Castle Howard. As Rosalind herself later made clear, this was actually wine which had gone off, condemned as so sour that "not even a dipsomaniac under the influence of his worst drink craving would have touched the mixture of fungus and smelly liquid". According to her daughter Dorothy's account, there was actually some good 'Hock' wine saved, which Rosalind gave to her elderly land agent, on the basis that he was" too old for it to matter". Beer, though, had been banned once the temperance cause was adopted. The produce of the Castle Howard brew house, including a particularly strong Audit Ale, had been poured down the drains.

In the second half of her life, Rosalind espoused three main causes – temperance reform, Home Rule for Ireland and women's suffrage. She lived to see two of the three partially achieved. The 1918 Representation of the People Act finally gave most women aged 30 and over the right to vote in parliamentary elections. With the voting age for men being reduced to 21, women were still not being treated equally, but a huge step towards equality of the sexes had been taken. A year later, Lady Astor became the first female Member of Parliament. We can only wonder what would have happened if Rosalind had been younger and in better health. Would she have considered standing for Parliament? Nancy Astor has a secure place in history but it's often forgotten that she too was an advocate for temperance. She helped steer a bill through parliament prohibiting the sale of intoxicants to the under 18s.

The Irish issue still continues to create division within both

Britain and Ireland. But after the Easter Rising of 1916, anti-British feeling was running very high. By 1920, Northern Ireland had a limited version of Home Rule and in the following year, the Irish Free State (later to become the Republic of Ireland) was formed.

To Rosalind's dismay, the vicissitudes of British politics and, ultimately, the First World War, meant that hopes for significant temperance reform remained unfulfilled. The power of the liquor trade, nationally, remained unbroken. She didn't support government control of the liquor trade so perhaps there is an irony that, as we shall see in the next chapter, this is exactly what happened in Carlisle itself during the war. But in her own way Rosalind did achieve much needed change. She fashioned the alcohol-ridden Cumberland estates into paragons of moderation. In doing so, she upset many but she also improved the quality of lives of many others. Nationally, she ensured women in the temperance movement maintained a high profile.

In her public roles even *The Times* had to concede that Rosalind "possessed to a remarkable degree the confidence of hundreds of thousands of organized women workers for Liberal and social causes, and she deserved it" – a grudging compliment, but a compliment nevertheless. It sums up the paradox of this remarkable woman. As her son-in-law, Charles Roberts, stated in *The Radical Countess, the History of the Life of Rosalind, Countess of Carlisle*, Rosalind Howard was "insufficiently appreciated by some, grossly maligned by others".

It is sad that she is remembered more for her temperament than for her temperance work.

Conclusion

Even before the end of the 19th century, the temperance movement had seen some successes. Non-drinkers now had a choice, especially if they went to the seaside. Temperance Hotels were set up in places as far afield as Bridlington and Bournemouth. The Temperance Hall became a familiar edifice in many towns, a community hub for a whole range of recreational and educational activities. Thomas Cook had sown the seeds of his successful travel agency organizing trips to temperance events.

There were even new towns and villages built specifically with no public houses; for example Temperance Town in Cardiff and Saltaire and Bourneville, specially built for factory workers. Sometimes, of course, this meant a proliferation of pubs just outside the perimeter. People weren't always so easily denied their pleasure.

The number of public houses actually declined in some areas as licences were not renewed. Women proved themselves particularly effective lobbying at the Brewsters sessions, when licences were considered. In *A Century of Service* commemorating 100 years of the BWTA, the scene is described, "The Trade applicants and their advocates would look askance, and sometimes apprehensive when a bevy of women, each wearing her White Ribbon badge, appeared in Court. Even though no word was said, their very presence demonstrated their opposition to the increase of drinking facilities." Sometimes one of the women would address the magistrates, pointing out that the premises were close to a school or in an area where there was already a proliferation of drinking establishments. They usually had a courteous reception, often a sympathetic one, from the magistrates.

The Police Court Missionary service, started by the Church of

England Temperance Society, was found to be so beneficial that it led to the creation of the probation service. As *A Century of Service*, the BWTA's anniversary booklet comments, "… here and overseas, a number of social aid schemes it [the temperance movement] was responsible for starting, have been taken up by civic or government authorities." Again this is often forgotten by historians today.

Had the Liberals' Licensing Bill of 1908 been passed, the temperance movement, though not the prohibition one, would have secured a great victory. The bill's aims were the ultimate reduction in licences by one third, payment of compensation for loss of a licence for 14 years after which the licence would revert to the state, the local option regarding the granting of new licences and restoration to the licensing justices of the right to impose conditions on licences.

The London County Council already effectively had a 'temperance policy'. As it acquired land for housing improvements or redevelopment, it would abandon the licences on the pubs which had come with the land. The council also controlled over 4,500 acres of open space where no beer was allowed in any refreshment room. Teetotalism and temperance were no longer the preserve of the north.

There was a huge amount of correspondence in the press about the proposed legislation which would have affected the whole of England. Official figures were published which showed that the number of licensed premises had decreased by over 500 in 1905, although in fact this was little over half a percent of the total. Statistics were used to show a correlation between the number of licensed premises per household and the number of convictions for drunkenness.

The bill got caught up in the struggle with the Conservative-dominated House of Lords over its veto over legislation. Lord Landsdowne led the House of Lords' revolt. Charles Roberts,

Rosalind Howard's son-in-law, comments that this decision "prevented the establishment of the veto of the people over the liquor trade; but that at least contributed to the loss by the Lords of their veto over legislation".

But the 1908 Licensing Bill was also defeated by vested interests. We might think this means the brewers and the publicans themselves but in fact many wealthy aristocrats had invested heavily in debentures secured upon their premises. Figures of £5 million to £100 million were bandied around. A powerful committee, chaired by Stanley Boulter, Chairman of the Law Debenture Corporation, had been set up to protect the interests of these debenture holders. The Committee argued it was "as solicitous as any members of the so-called Temperance Party for the prevention of immoderate and excessive drinking, and would willingly support any reasonable and practical measure having that object". Rather hollow words in the context of its mission. This influential Committee had "been formed not to resist temptation, but to resist proposals of confiscation which could lead to the annihilation of an immense amount of capital".

The Archbishop of Canterbury was taken to task for supporting the Licensing Bill. There was "nothing temperate about temperance societies", he was told; they were "inspired by fanatical hatred of alcoholic beverages". This was a very uncharitable condemnation of the motives of the many religious men and women who championed the temperance cause, having seen at first hand the problems alcohol abuse created. Some wealthy individuals even threatened to withdraw their subscriptions to charities and church organizations if the bishops supported the proposed legislation. Greed and fear won the day. The bill was rejected.

Official support for the temperance cause from the established church had often waivered. But many individuals and evangelists, as well as the Salvation Army, had no qualms in linking temperance to salvation.

If women had had the vote at this time, would they have been able to influence the progress of the proposed legislation? It is naive to think so. Those vested interests were very powerful and it would be a long time before either House of Parliament would come even remotely close to having enough female members to exert any pressure upon their male counterparts.

Charles Roberts went on to write that in his view the opportunity for significant reform had been lost in 1907 when the Prime Minister had offered to push for minor licensing reforms with the promise of greater ones in the future. His mother-in-law, Rosalind, strongly disagreed. There could be no compromise in her mind. But in reality Charles was right. The chance had been lost. Irish MPs then demanded that the issue of licensing reform take second place to the establishment of Home Rule in Ireland.

In 1914, fearing that drunkenness would undermine the war effort, the government took powers to take over the drink industry in areas where they thought it necessary, for example where there were armament factories. In reality they didn't use these powers as much as one might have expected. A system of state control was introduced in Enfield, another in Scotland. On April 6th, 1915, King George V signed the temperance pledge for the duration of the war.

The most significant area where state control was implemented was Carlisle; it had both a naval base and a new arms factory at nearby Gretna. Carlisle city centre had over 100 pubs. These, together with the four local breweries, were taken under government control. A Liquor Control Board was established. Three of the four breweries and 50 licensed premises were closed. Great efforts were made to improve the remaining pubs, with separate areas for women and space for games and other recreational pursuits. Responsible drinking became the order of the day. All internal and external advertisements for alcohol were banned. Under the 'no treating' policy, customers could no longer buy rounds.

The Licensing Act of 1921 abolished the Liquor Control Board but the Carlisle and District State Management Scheme took over responsibility in the city.

There were serious discussions about extending state control throughout the country but Lloyd George, who had initially championed the idea, became frustrated that the brewers were making too many demands for there to be a sustainable agreement.

The brewers didn't like the Carlisle experiment, as it became known. Neither did the prohibitionists. They didn't want any drink trade, regardless of whether it was controlled by the industry itself or by the government.

Other temperance reformers did welcome it and argued that it had significantly reduced drunkenness in the area. This argument was countered by a blunt retort in the House of Commons debate in 1920. "Carlisle was always a sober town. Now it is more than a sober town. It is a dismal one."

The experiment proved a surprisingly long one. For in Carlisle state control of the drink industry actually continued right up until the 1970s. It was only as denationalization became the new political creed that the Carlisle pubs were sold into private ownership.

The First World War changed Britain, and the world, forever. The country united against a common foe. Women proved by their actions that they were equal partners with men to save the country. Their contribution to the war effort couldn't be denied. Actions had spoken louder than words. Most of the women featured in this book supported the call for women to have the vote. At last, in 1918, this object was achieved, at least to a limited extent.

Some academics argue that women temperance campaigners diluted their case too much by linking it to a call for women's suffrage. I would argue the opposite. We see strong-willed females who were anything but narrow-minded. They saw social problems all around them and they couldn't tackle one without highlighting, at least, many others. Those who rose to prominence on the temperance platform had an opportunity, some would say a duty, to speak about women's rights, as well as their roles and responsibilities. The campaigns for suffrage and temperance were natural bed-fellows.

History has a selective memory. Demands for social change come and go out of fashion. Women's rights are still fashionable, so the suffragettes are seen as heroines of their time. It is often forgotten that there were many women, like some featured in this book, who abhorred the violent protests of the suffragettes yet campaigned peaceably for the right to vote. Without doubt, fighting the temperance cause proved empowering for women.

In today's society, the call for temperance is just a very small voice. The current exhortation to "Drink Responsibly" (itself a somewhat mixed message) is about as far as the alcohol industry, and any British government, is likely to go to promote moderation in drinking habits. And the problem of defining 'moderation' still exists.

As this book shows, the temperance movement produced many heroines. They didn't allow themselves to be broken by scandal or ridicule. Their work is still worthy of our attention and it should not just be the feminists or the teetotallers of today who find much to admire in their stories.

Let's leave a pioneering woman, one of the first female doctors, with the last word:

To Drink Or Not To Drink

A PARODY

BY DR KATE MITCHELL

To drink or not to drink, that is the question;
Whether 'tis nobler to abstain, and suffer
The taunts and insults of our drinking neighbours
Or to take wine with them and shun the duty
Of setting good example. To die, – to live, –
In health, and by our life to say we make
The effort to attain the highest virtue
That flesh can aim at – 'tis a consummation
Devoutly to be wished. To die, – to live, –
To live! Perchance to drink; ay, there's the rub,
For in that drinking life what crimes occur
When men have shuffled off their reason's guide
Must give us pause. For 'tis the wine
That makes calamity of so long life …

From *The British Women's Temperance Journal* January **1884**

Sources and Bibliography

I have taken a deliberate decision not to interrupt the narrative of this book with footnotes.

My main sources, primary and secondary, are set out below. Anyone wishing further information about the source of particular information or quote is welcome to contact me through my website www.rosblackcreative.com

Special note: The word "teetotaller" is now more commonly spelt with two 'l's but in some quotes it appears with just one, as was the practice at the time.

Archives

British Library
British Newspaper Archives
Castle Howard Archives
Eastnor Castle Archives
Lambeth Palace Archives
Institute of Alcohol Studies Archives
Joseph Livesey Collection, University of Lancashire
National British Women's Total Abstinence Union Archives
Portsmouth History Centre
Plymouth & West Devon Record Office
Plymouth Local Studies Library
Salvation Army International Heritage Centre
Surrey History Centre

Annual Reports, Minutes and Conference Papers

Band of Hope Union
British Women's Temperance Association
Church of England Temperance Society
National British Women's Temperance Association
National Temperance League
Royal Sailors' Rests
Women's Total Abstinence Union
United Kingdom Alliance

Historical newspapers and periodicals

Alliance News
Band of Hope Review
British Temperance Advocate
British Women's Temperance Journal
Onward
Portsmouth Evening News
The Blackburn Standard
The Blackburn Times
The Bluejacket
The Hampshire Telegraph
The Hastings & St Leonards Observer
The Illustrated London News
The Irish Times
The Manchester Guardian
The Pall Mall Gazette
The Saturday Review
The Teetotaler Journal
The Temperance Record

The Times
The Weekly Record (NTL Journal)
War Cry
Western Temperance Herald
Wings
Women's Signal

Books and articles

Barrow, Margaret *Thesis – Temperate feminists: The British Women's Temperance Association 1870 – 1914* (1999)

Black, Ros *A Talent for Humanity – The Life and Work of Lady Henry Somerset* (2010)

Black, Ros *Duxhurst – Surrey's Lost Village* (2011)

Bordin, Ruth *Women and Temperance: The Quest for Power and Liberty 1873 – 1900* (Philadelphia 1981)

Blocker, Fahey & Tyrell *Alcohol and Temperance In Modern History*

Booth, Catherine *Reminiscences* (transcribed by DM Bennett 2005)

Booth, Catherine *Papers on Practical Religion* (1879)

Booth, William *How to Reach the Masses*

Booth, William *In Darkest England and The Way Out* (1890)

Booth-Tucker, Frederick *The Life of Catherine Booth*

Chappell, Jennie *Noble Work by Noble Women* (London 1900)

Church of England Temperance Society Jubilee Book (1887)

Cohen, Susan *The Salvation Army* (2013)

Dictionary of National Biography

Dolling, Father Robert *Ten Years in a Portsmouth Slum* (1896)

Every Woman's Encyclopedia Volume 1

Fitzpatrick, Kathleen *Lady Henry Somerset* (1923)

Fletcher, JMJ *Mrs Wightman of Shrewsbury* (1906)

Furtado, Peter *Quakers* (2013)

Gifford, Carolyn De Swarte *Writing Out My heart – Selections from the Journal of Frances E Willard* (Illinois 1995)

Gifford, Carolyn De Swarte and Slagell, Amy R *Let Something Good Be said – Speeches and Writings of Frances E Willard* (2007)

Gordon, Anna A *The Beautiful Life of Frances E Willard* (Chicago 1898)

Gray, Todd *Remarkable Women of Devon* (2009)

Greenaway, J *Drink and British Politics since 1830* (Basingstoke 2003)

Gulliver, Doris *Dame Agnes Weston* (London 1971)

Harrison, Brian *Drink and the Victorians, The Temperance Question in England 1815 – 1872* (London 1971)

Hattersley, Roy *Blood & Fire – William and Catherine Booth and their Salvation Army* (1999)

Henley, Lady Dorothy *Rosalind Howard, Countess of Carlisle* (London 1958)

Hopkins, JC *Active Service or Miss Sarah Robinson's work among our Sailors* (1872)

Kingston, WHG *A Yacht Voyage Round England* (1879)

Longford, Elizabeth *Eminent Victorian Women* (London/New York 1981)

Moss WE *The Life of Mrs Lewis* (London 1926)

National British Women's Total Abstinence Union *A Century of Service 1876 – 1976*

Niessen, Olwen Claire *Aristocracy, Temperance and Social Reform – the life of Lady Henry Somerset* (London/New York 2007)

Paxman, Jeremy *The Victorians* (2009)

Roberts, C *The Radical Countess* (Carlisle 1962)

Robinson, Sarah *Christianity and Teetotalism A Voice from the Army* (1876)

Robinson, Sarah *Yarns* (1892)

Robinson, Sarah *A Life Record* (1898)

Robinson, Sarah *My Book* (1914)

Rowntree, Joseph and Sherwell, Arthur *The Temperance Problem* (London 1899)

Shiman, Lilian Lewis *Crusade against Drink in Victorian England* (New York 1988)

Smith, Frederick, edited by *The Jubilee of the Band of Hope Movement* (London 1897)

Somerset, Lady Henry *Our Village Life* (1884)

Somerset, Lady Henry *Sketches in Black and White* (London 1896)

Somerset, Lady Henry *Under the Arch of Life* (London 1906)

Somerset, Lady Henry *Beauty for Ashes* (London 1913)

Surtees, Virginia *The Artist and the Autocrat George and Rosalind Howard Earl and Countess of Carlisle* (Salisbury 1988)

Tomkinson, EM *Sarah Robinson, Agnes Weston, Mrs Meredith* (1887)

Tyrell, Ian *Woman's World – WCTU in International Perspective 1880 – 1930* (Carolina 1991)

Ward, Audrey *Discovering Reigate Priory – the Places and the People* (1998)

Weston, Agnes *My Life among the Blue-Jackets* (London 1909)

Wightman, Julia *Haste to the Rescue* (London 1860)

Willard, Frances *Do Everything: A Handbook for White Ribboners* (Chicago 1895)

Winskill, PT *Temperance Standard Bearers of the Nineteenth Century* (Liverpool 1898)

Winskill, Peter *The Temperance Movement* Volume 3

Wintz, Sophia (edited by) *Ashore & Afloat*

Witts, Florence *Frances E Willard – The Story of a Noble Woman* (London)

Wojtczak, Helena *Women in Victorian Sussex*

Index